THE QUEEN

ALLEN LANE

ALLEN LANE

Penguin Books Ltd, 17 Grosvenor Gardens, London s w 1 w o b d

—

First published 1977

—

—

I S B N 0 7139 1060 7

—

Printed in Great Britain by
Richard Clay (The Chaucer Press) Ltd,
Bungay, Suffolk

Contents

List of Plates

7. THE QUEEN AS HEAD OF STATE
   (a) The State Opening of Parliament, 1958 (Paul Popper Ltd)
   (b) The Queen at her desk, Balmoral Castle, 1972 (Paul Popper Ltd)

8. WITH HER PRIME MINISTER
   (a) Sir Winston Churchill after dinner at 10 Downing Street, 1955 (Keystone Press Agency Ltd)
   (b) Sir Harold Wilson at Downing Street, 1976 (Keystone Press Agency Ltd)

9. ROYAL DUTIES
   (a) Trooping the Colour, 1963 (Paul Popper Ltd)
   (b) A banquet in São Paulo, Brazil, 1968 (Paul Popper Ltd)
   (c) With the Yeomen of the Guard, July 1974 (Syndication International)
   (d) Inspecting the parade, Sovereign's Company, First Grenadier Guard, 1953 (Paul Popper Ltd)
   (e) New Zealand, 1970 (Camera Press Ltd)
   (f) With Canadian Indian chiefs and their wives, 1976 (Syndication International)
   (g) Invested as a bard, 1946 (Paul Popper Ltd)
   (h) Visiting Glasgow's new Fruit Market, 1969 (Paul Popper Ltd)

10. MEETING THE PEOPLE
    (a) Aberfan after the disaster, 1966 (Paul Popper Ltd)
    (b) At Silverwood Colliery, South Yorkshire, 1975 (Syndication International)
    (c) With the oldest Chelsea Pensioner, 1975 (Syndication International)
    (d) Australia, 1970 (Camera Press Ltd)

11. RESPONSES TO MONARCHY
    (a) Coronation souvenirs, 1952 (Paul Popper Ltd)
    (b) Glasgow, 1953 (Syndication International)
    (c) Royal tour of Nigeria, 1956 (Camera Press Ltd)
    (d) Stirling University, 1972 (The Scotsman Publications Ltd)

12. Badminton, 1972 (Paul Popper Ltd)

The Opening of Parliament

The Chamber lights are dimmed, then glow again
On ermine robes, Orders of Chivalry,
Dress uniforms, and wigs, and white lawn sleeves,
Long evening gowns, and costly jewellery.

The Cap of Maintenance, the Sword of State
Carried in front of her – with careful tread
Dressed all in white and silver, comes the Queen;
The Imperial Crown is heavy on her head.

Four pages lift and spread the crimson train
As, handed by the Duke, she mounts the throne;
And, even in this glittering company,
Admiring eyes are turned to her alone.

Her faithful Commons, summoned by Black Rod
Come through the corridors and stand to hear;
The Chancellor presents the Gracious Speech;
She reads the legislation for the year.

She tells of journeys over land and sea
Through burning heat and cold, that she will make –
So many people pressing near to her
To see her smile; so many hands to shake.

They love her for her wisdom and her pride,
Her friendship and her quiet majesty.
And soon the streets of Britain will be thronged
With crowds rejoicing in her Jubilee.

11

The Queen

But as the cool, unfaltering voice reads on,
A different picture forms upon the air –
A small, quick figure walking all alone
Across a glen studded with standing deer.

The wind blows freshly from the mountain-tops,
Brown water stands in pools among the peat;
She whistles all the labradors to heel;
The heather crunches stiff beneath her feet.

She sees the swallows wheeling in the sky,
The firs reflected, trembling, in the loch;
The cairns of stone upon the nearer hills,
White flash of waterfalls upon black rock.

She notes a crumbling wall, an open gate;
With countrywoman's eyes she views the scene;
Yet, walking free upon her own estate –
Still, in her solitude, she is the Queen.

The Queen and the Constitution

THE constitutional status of the monarchy is curiously little understood. Eleven years ago in a survey of public opinion on the usual sampling basis two questions were asked. If the views of the Queen on a matter of policy conflicted with those of the Prime Minister, which *would* prevail and which *should*? A substantial majority not only believed that the Queen's opinion would prevail, but also that it should. There has not been any recent research into the matter, but the general contempt in which politicians are held has not become less over the last decade, nor is there much evidence to suggest that the British public has become better informed about the working of its own constitution.

Yet a reading of the most elementary text books on constitutional law and history would show how inaccurate is this version of the relationship between the Crown and its ministers. In the reign of George III the monarchy still possessed real power. The younger Pitt depended for his position as Prime Minister upon the support of the King. Fox was in the political wilderness for long years precisely because the King detested him. His great hope of recovery lay not so much in electoral or parliamentary defeat of the Crown as in the chance that the King would go permanently mad and Fox's close friend the Prince of Wales would become Regent. Eventually he did, but Fox was dead by then and the Prince anyway decided to double-cross the Whigs.

It is not easy to fix an exact date when the power of the

Crown to make and unmake ministries finally disappeared. It had certainly gone by the early years of Queen Victoria, and Bagehot's celebrated summary of the situation has been broadly true ever since he wrote in 1867: 'The sovereign has, under a constitutional monarchy such as ours, three rights – the right to be consulted, the right to encourage, the right to warn'. Queen Victoria tried to interfere in political matters long after that, to an extent which a modern monarch would scarcely imitate, but she could not get her way against a Prime Minister and Cabinet really determined on a particular course. This was equally true of her successors, who wisely did not seek to exercise powers which were clearly becoming obsolete.

The function of the Queen today can be divided into that of influence and that of power. Influence is an intangible and indefinable element. It not only includes Bagehot's three 'rights', it also includes an almost magical symbolism of the permanence and unity of the nation. As Mr Ian Gilmour writes*

Popular craving for mystery, colour and pageantry can be satisfied by royalty. The monarch is a person and a symbol. He makes power and the state both intelligible and mysterious. Presidents make them neither. Legitimacy, the acceptance by the governed of a political system, is far better aided by an ancient monarchy set above the political battle than by a transient president who has gained his position through that battle ... Modern societies still need myth and ritual. A monarch and his family supply it; there is no magic about a mud-stained politician.

This is, of course, something which one either feels or does not. You can never argue with someone who says that the Queen is just a person like anyone else and that the mystique of royalty is a piece of meaningless mumbo-jumbo. All you can say in reply is that a very large proportion of citizens in

* *The Body Politic*, 1969, p. 313.

the countries where the monarchy has remained above politics feel differently, and obtain a deep sense of satisfaction from that feeling. The immense popularity of the Queen on her visits to France and the United States suggests that, even in those nations which have not, as it were, separated pomp from power and which confer on the head of state an active political role, there is nevertheless a deep nostalgia for the sort of sentiments aroused by monarchy. 'You have the Queen,' an American once said, 'We have only the Flag'.

That, then, is one aspect of the influence of the monarchy – and it is probably the most important of all. Another aspect is the triple function mentioned by Bagehot. By the nature of things it is not at all easy to discover how far the monarch's undoubted right to be consulted, to encourage and to warn actually affects events. It is a reasonable assumption that a King or Queen with a good memory and long experience can draw a Prime Minister's attention to past parallels with present problems and point out possible snags in particular proposals. It is also a reasonable assumption that any Prime Minister of sense will pay some attention to what is said even if he does not agree. At the very least he will take good care when he consults the monarch to be very well briefed and to know his case thoroughly. George VI, his biographer writes, 'was aware that in his talks with ministers he was not infrequently successful in presenting arguments which caused them to reconsider decisions at which they had already arrived'.

Such talks are, of course, confidential at the time and it is only many years later that some record may be made available to a royal biographer. Yet records can be fallible, and even if the conversation is accurately reported there may be no way of knowing just what effect it has had on the minister concerned. It is therefore not easy to cite specific instances of royal arguments prevailing even when the documents have been published. It is of course impossible to do this for any episodes in the life of Queen Elizabeth II, for her discussions with ministers are rightly veiled in confidentiality. One would, for example, like to know how fully she was informed about Anthony Eden's plans for the Suez operation of 1956 and, if she was so informed, what she thought about them. But very properly the facts about this and many other episodes will not be made available during the present reign.

The most which can be said is that no Prime Minister is likely to disregard a warning from someone with the Queen's long experience of politics. To quote Bagehot again: 'Supposing the King to be right and to have what Kings often have, the gift of effectual expression, he could not help moving his Minister. He might not always turn his course, but he would always trouble his mind.' The influence of the monarch over the ministers by whose advice he or she is formally bound may not be easy to define or specify, but no one should assume from this that it does not exist.

The Crown has power as well as influence, but the vast majority of its powers are not real powers in the sense that the Queen can actually of her own initiative appoint an ambassador or confer a peerage or make an order-in-council. The Crown constantly figures in official documents, but in nearly every case what the Crown does is done on the 'advice' of a minister, and that 'advice' if pressed, in spite of argument or counter-suggestions, is binding.

Not all the advice necessarily comes from members of the British Cabinet. It is worth remembering that the Queen is not only Queen of Great Britain, but also Queen of the Commonwealth monarchies such as Australia, New Zealand, Canada and several others. She is represented in those countries by a Governor-General and her communications go through him. The government of a Commonwealth monarchy would strongly object to the British Cabinet as such having any say in its affairs.

During the Australian constitutional crisis of autumn

1975, which culminated in the Governor-General, Sir John Kerr, dismissing the Prime Minister, Mr Gough Whitlam, all communications went direct from Sir John to the Queen via her Private Secretary. The British government was not involved at all. The Governor-General acted, as was proper, entirely on his own initiative. He simply kept the Queen informed. What would have happened if Mr Whitlam had got his blow in first and advised the Queen to dismiss Sir John? It would not have been an easy problem, but the answer probably is that she would have felt obliged to accept the advice. Fortunately the question did not arise.

Admittedly there are certain powers which the Queen can exercise without being advised by a minister. She can create Knights of the Garter, the Thistle and the Patrick. She can confer the Order of Merit, and the various degrees of the Victorian Order from the GCVO downwards are in her personal gift. She also appoints her own Private Secretary and most of the officers of the household, although one or two still remain political and change with the government.

These, however, are in terms of the running of the country relatively minor powers. Are there any major matters still left in which the Queen can act on her personal responsibility? In theory the Queen can appoint or dismiss ministers, dissolve Parliament, veto a Bill and indeed do a large number of drastic things. In practice there are really only two fields in which some slight degree of personal discretion still survives: the appointment of a Prime Minister and the dissolution of Parliament. Let us take each in turn.

The appointment of the Prime Minister is the more important of the two. The reason why the Queen cannot avoid an element of personal responsibility here is because this is the one act which by definition she cannot accept on formal and binding 'advice', for the simple reason that there is no one there to give it. The appointment has to be made when a Prime Minister either dies or resigns. No Prime Minister has actually died in office since Palmerston in 1865, but the two situations are constitutionally much the same. When a Prime Minister resigns, he is no longer in a position to take responsibility for the advice he gives and thus shield the monarch from parliamentary and public criticism. Moreover, in certain circumstances of resignation, for example, after defeat at a general election, it would be peculiarly absurd if the outgoing Prime Minister could give 'binding' advice to the Queen about whom to appoint from the party which has just defeated him.

The Queen's first consideration, whether the Prime Minister has resigned because of ill health, or a feeling that he has had enough or electoral defeat, must be to appoint the man or woman who can command a majority in the House of Commons. This is the essential prerequisite for a Prime Minister. In all normal circumstances he or she will be the leader of the party which has won the largest number of seats. In the case of a Prime Minister's resignation after losing a general election the obvious course is to send for the leader of the party which has won it, or, if no one has 'won', the leader of the party with the largest number of seats in the House, for example, Sir Harold Wilson after the election of February 1974.

The problem for the Queen has not been quite so simple and straightforward when a Prime Minister at the head of his party with a majority in the House has retired between general elections. In these circumstances there is no reason against her asking the advice of the outgoing Prime Minister, but such advice cannot be 'binding' and the final responsibility must be hers. The first occasion in her reign when this situation occurred was after Sir Winston Churchill's resignation in April 1955. The Conservative party did not possess any system of election to the leadership when the party was in power. In opposition they would have had to devise a method. There would, for example, have been some sort of intra-party ballot for the leadership in the Commons in 1911, if Austen Chamberlain and Walter Long had not decided to withdraw in favour of the 'dark horse', the third runner, Bonar Law, in order to minimize conflict and allow a walk-over to a compromise candidate. A similar *nem. con.* election took place in 1921 when Bonar Law retired for the time being and Austen Chamberlain took his place. It so happened, however, that for the next forty-four years the Conservative leadership only changed when the party was in office. The Conservatives were content to leave the process of selection to the royal prerogative of choosing a new Prime Minister. During the same period the Labour leadership changed no less than five times, always in opposition and therefore by an election within the parliamentary party.

The effect of the Conservative tradition was to put a considerable responsibility upon the Queen. It is true that there was no problem in 1955; Anthony Eden had long been regarded as the inevitable successor; any other choice would have been thought absurd. It was a different matter when serious illness in the aftermath of the Suez crisis unexpectedly obliged Eden himself to resign in January 1957. There was not a self-evident successor, and, although the Press commentators, with the notable exception of the late Randolph Churchill, assumed that R. A. Butler would be the man, strong support existed in the party for Harold Macmillan. Queen Victoria, confronted by a similar choice after Gladstone's resignation early in 1894, made no inquiries of the Liberal party nor did she consult Gladstone. She sent for Lord Rosebery simply because she thought he would be a better Prime Minister than the rival claimant, Sir William Harcourt, whom she particularly disliked and distrusted. In 1923, when Bonar Law resigned, King George V, having to choose between Lord Curzon and Stanley Baldwin, was not prepared to act in quite such a peremptory manner. He would have sought Bonar Law's advice if the latter had been well enough to give it. Instead he consulted, through his private secretary, various elder statesmen, and his choice fell on Baldwin. There is not much doubt that Baldwin would have been the party's choice too.

In January 1957 the Cabinet decided, after both Butler and Macmillan had left the room, that Lord Salisbury and Lord Kilmuir (who, because they were peers, were regarded as ineligible themselves) should see each member separately and ask him which of the two he preferred. The verdict of the Cabinet was overwhelmingly for Macmillan. Inquiries were also made in the upper echelons of the party's parliamentary and national organization. These yielded the same result. Lord Salisbury delivered his findings to the Queen. Sir Winston Churchill also had an audience at which, as he somewhat improperly announced in his election address in 1959, he recommended Macmillan. It is often said that Anthony Eden was not consulted. There is good reason to believe that in fact he was, though he has been more discreet than Sir Winston about revealing the nature of his advice. The Queen accordingly sent for Harold Macmillan. Although there was a section of the party which would have preferred Butler, it is clear that they were a minority. An elective system, as in the case of Baldwin thirty-four years earlier, would almost certainly have produced the same answer.

One cannot be quite so sure that this would have been the case on the second occasion when the Queen was faced with a decision about the succession. Macmillan's sudden illness and announcement of resignation in the middle of the Conservative Conference at Blackpool in October 1963 occurred before the expiry of the period within which under recent legislation a peer could decide whether or not to renounce his peerage. Lord Hailsham announced, perhaps almost too aggressively, his intention to take advantage of this provision and challenge the obvious front runner – R. A. Butler again. In the event Lord Home was persuaded after some hesitation to disclaim his peerage too, and, after a fairly full consultation with the various elements in the party hierarchy, Macmillan recommended the Queen to invite him to find out whether he could form an administration. He found that he could, and was duly appointed as Prime Minister but, if there had been an elective system, it is not certain that Lord Home would have allowed himself to be a runner at all. He was acceptable in the sense that scarcely anyone was against him, whereas there were very strong feelings, pro and anti, regarding Butler and Hailsham, but it is not obvious how this particular result could have been achieved by an election even if Lord Home had stood.

However that may be, the discontent in the party was much greater than it had been in 1957. There was widespread criticism, not of the Queen personally, but of a system by which it seemed possible for a small group of Tory grandees – 'a magic circle', as the phrase went – to fix the succession without much regard to the party generally. This appearance was given a certain plausibility by the fact that the Queen had formally consulted on each occasion very few people: in 1957 only Lord Salisbury who was quite undeservedly described as 'the Kingmaker', Sir Winston and perhaps Eden; in 1963 only Macmillan. In reality a great deal of consultation had gone on at one remove behind the scenes, and no doubt the documents will show that the Queen was fully aware of these. But in retrospect one could perhaps say that it would have been better if she had directly invited the opinions of, say, the chief whip, the chairman of the party, the chairman of the 1922 committee and one or two other prominent persons as well as those whom she did consult. Consultation would thus have not only taken place, but been seen to have taken place.

It is, however, unlikely that the Queen will be faced in future with the problem of choice in this sort of situation. The Labour party has long made it clear that it would not expect anyone to accept the premiership unless he or she had first been elected as leader by the parliamentary Labour party. This was what happened when James Callaghan succeeded Sir Harold Wilson in March 1976. The discontent within the Conservative party, which arose from the events of 1963, has resulted in the establishment of the electoral system under which Heath was elected in 1965 and under which, with slight modifications, Mrs Thatcher was elected in 1975. So far it has only operated when the party has been in opposition, but presumably the same method would apply if a Conservative Prime Minister resigned or died between general elections. In these circumstances the Queen's choice is effectively narrowed to that of endorsing a party election.

Is there nowadays any conceivable situation in which the Queen might have to exercise her discretion in appointing a Prime Minister? To say no would be rash. Obviously such a situation will be highly abnormal and will occur very rarely, but this is not to say that it could never occur in any imaginable circumstances. Mr John Grigg in an interesting article in the *Spectator* (4 December 1976) raised the question of the exercise of the Queen's prerogative in the event of the Prime Minister resigning because he found himself in a minority in the Cabinet over the measures needed to secure credit from the International Monetary Fund. The fragility of the pound might have made a general election impossible for the time being – or at any rate highly inexpedient. Should the Queen send for Mrs Thatcher as leader of the next largest party in the House of Commons? Or should she exercise a royal initiative by seeking agreement on some sort of coalition? Or should she either ask Mr Callaghan to stay on until the Labour party had elected a leader whom she could then appoint as Prime Minister, or alternatively herself appoint an interim Prime Minister pending such an election? Mr Grigg thought she should take one of the variants of the third course. King George V in an analogous situation in 1931 took the second course and, if it had failed, would have taken the first. The interesting constitutional point, however, is not so much what would have been the right choice – on which there could be much argument – but rather the existence of any choice at all.

There can be little doubt that in certain conditions of emergency an element of real discretion in the exercise of the prerogative of appointing the Prime Minister still exists. The potential situation outlined by Mr Grigg is one example. It is possible to think of others in which recourse to an intra-party election would not be the only solution. Three times in the twentieth century – Lloyd George in 1916, MacDonald in 1931, Churchill in 1940 – Prime Ministers who had no likelihood of being elected immediately (and in one case of ever being elected) to the leadership of their parties were appointed in circumstances of emergency. Who can say for certain that such circumstances will never recur?

The obverse of appointment is dismissal. It is scarcely conceivable that the Sovereign would nowadays dismiss a Prime Minister unless the latter went mad or suffered some similar catastrophe. In 1834 William IV in effect dismissed Melbourne, but no subsequent monarch has imitated his action. The crisis in Australia at the end of 1975 arose from a constitutional set-up which has no parallel in Britain. The Senate, which has co-equal powers with the Lower House, refused supply in order to force Mr Whitlam to call an election. Mr Whitlam declined to do so. Whether or not Sir John Kerr was right to break the deadlock by sacking the Prime Minister and replacing him by someone who would recommend a dissolution will long be argued. The situation could not arise in Britain where the Upper House cannot touch finance at all and has only a limited power of delay over other legislation.

The other discretionary prerogative is the right to dissolve Parliament. It is generally accepted that the Queen cannot force a dissolution against the wishes of the Prime Minister. There is no instance of this occurring in modern times. But does the converse apply? Must she always accept the advice of the Prime Minister if he requests a dissolution? There is no recent precedent in Britain for refusal, although it is known that in 1924 King George V would have refused it to Ramsay MacDonald, who was head of a minority government, if he had not already ascertained that neither Asquith nor Baldwin was willing to take office in the circumstances. There is, however, more than one instance in the Dominions. In Canada in 1926 the Governor-General, Lord Byng, refused a dissolution to Mackenzie King, and in South Africa Sir Patrick Duncan on the outbreak of war in 1939 took the same action when asked for a dissolution by General Herzog. The success of the manoeuvre depends on the Crown or its representative being able to find an alternative Prime Minister who can carry on without himself having to call for a dissolution almost at once; otherwise the original refusal is bound to seem unfair to the previous Prime Minister. Byng was not able to do this, but Duncan – thanks to divisions within the majority party – was.

The point has not arisen directly during the reign of the present Queen, but there was a certain amount of discussion in the press and elsewhere after the general election of February 1974. As in 1924 no party had an absolute majority in the House. What would have happened if Sir Harold Wilson had been defeated, as was possible arithmetically, on the Address in reply to the Queen's Speech and had requested another dissolution within a few weeks of the previous one? Was the Queen bound to agree, or could she have invited Mr Heath back to try his hand at forming a government? Sir Harold behaved as though he were quite confident that a dissolution would be granted if he asked for it, and he seems to have convinced the Conservatives. But he was bound to appear confident. It does not follow that he was, or if he was, that he was right. In the event he was not defeated and every month that passed strengthened his claim to have a general election when the thought the moment to be right.

The discussion in the press prompted the *Tribune* group on 25 March to raise the matter with the Leader of the House, Mr Edward Short. They claimed that the Prime Minister had an 'absolute right to decide the date of the election, following discussion with his Cabinet colleagues'. Mr Short took his time to reply, and one can guess that there had been very careful legal consultation before he did. He was not prepared to accept the *Tribune* doctrine. He wrote on 9 May

Constitutional lawyers of the highest authority are of the clear opinion that the Sovereign is not in all circumstances bound to grant a Prime Minister's request for a dissolution. But the exercise of the royal prerogative in this matter is not determined only by past constitutional usages and precedents: the relevance of those usages and precedents has to be considered in relation to the actual circumstances.

Efforts to raise the matter in the House came to nothing, and there has been no controversy since. The *Tribune* claim is of course ridiculous as worded. What would the group have expected the Queen to do if Mr Heath, instead of resigning after his narrow defeat, had asked at once for a second general election on the off-chance that it might reverse the result of the first one? In practice, of course, the likelihood of the Queen refusing a dissolution is remote because the likelihood of a Prime Minister asking for it in circumstances which would warrant a refusal is equally remote. But the reserve power remains. The Queen could refuse. The most probable occasion – and it is not very probable – for the Queen to do so would be if she were asked for a dissolution by the head of a minority government very soon after the previous election and at a moment when a renewed contest might obviously be detrimental to the national interest, for example in the event of an economic crisis or imminent war. Even so, she would have to reckon on the Prime Minister's resignation and be reasonably certain that some other combination could be found to carry on the government with the existing Parliament. Minority governments are rare in modern British history. There have only been three since 1918. It is hard to imagine circumstances in which the Queen would refuse a dissolution to the head of a majority government, unless his party were breaking up – in which case he would not really be head of a majority government. Finally, one should emphasize that in all these hypothetical cases what is being suggested is not that the Queen must refuse a dissolution, merely that she could legitimately exercise her discretion to do so.

The Queen is the guardian of constitutional legitimacy in the broadest sense of the words. She cannot be this without possessing, in addition to influence and prestige however great, some ultimate powers of last resort. In Mr Ian Gilmour's words: 'The prerogative has always contained an element of emergency power, and unquestionably some emergency power remains in the Sovereign personally as opposed to the Crown.' Obviously this would only be exercised in a crisis of the most serious nature. Let us suppose that a government whether of the extreme left or right decided to perpetuate itself in power by repealing the provision in the Parliament Act which provides that a Parliament must be dissolved within five years of its election. This is the only piece of legislation on which the House of Lords can exercise an absolute veto, as opposed to mere delay. Probably it would use its veto, but a government resolved on an unconstitutional course could get round this by creating enough peers to carry the measure – several hundred if necessary. Surely that would be an occasion for the exercise of emergency powers. The Queen could refuse to create the peers; or, if by methods of bribery or intimidation the House of Lords had been bullied into submission without the need to create peers, she could revive the royal veto which has not been used since the reign of Queen Anne. She could moreover dismiss the Prime Minister and insist on a dissolution.

Clearly, if matters had reached this pass, we would be in the sort of situation prophesied by the famous 'monetarist', Professor Milton Friedman, who in an American television programme on 29 November 1976 declared that he saw the prospect of British economic collapse leading to a totalitarian state. Most of us would regard the prophecy as fantastic, and the prophet as ill-advised to depart from economics into futurology. Nevertheless the fantastic can sometimes become reality. If circumstances occurred which obliged the Queen to act in the way just described, Britain would be on the verge of revolution or civil war. But the Queen's action might just tip the balance towards legitimacy, or, if the potential dictator refused to accept dismissal and sought to destroy the monarchy, it would starkly reveal the illegal nature of his regime. Dictators attach importance to legitimacy. Hitler owed much of his acceptance to the fact that he became Chancellor by constitutional means. If Victor Emmanuel had been prepared to act against Mussolini, he might or might not have succeeded, but, if he had lost the throne, Mussolini's regime would have been that much less acceptable.

We are talking in terms of very remote contingencies. It is in the highest degree unlikely that this ultimate weapon will ever have to be used. In all normal conditions such an exercise of the royal prerogative would be 'unconstitutional'. Only the most extreme crisis would justify 'unconstitutional' action in order to preserve the constitution. Let us hope that the occasion never arises. If it did, it would portend the finish of the Britain we know, but it is just possible that the Britain we know could in that event be saved by the Sovereign.

DONALD HORNE

The Queen as Queen of Australia

IT seemed the ordinary Australian football crowd you get at
an international match: ready to shout down the visiting side
right from the kick-off, but prepared before then to display
true sportsmanship for a minute or two by remaining silent
during the playing of the visitors' national anthem. Not this
time. The visitors were British; when 'God Save the Queen'
began, a large part of the crowd booed. They weren't booing
Britain, however; 'God Save the Queen' used to be Australia's
only national anthem and they thought it was again being
played as such. When 'Advance Australia Fair' came on, they
settled down to the pleasures of more orthodox partisanship.

This anecdote illustrates the way the once apparently in-
violable political consensus in the Australia of which Elizabeth is Queen has been shaken (whether justly or not is
another matter) by the action on 11 November 1975 of the
vice-regal representative of Elizabeth in her role as Queen of
Australia. When Governor-General John Kerr dismissed
Gough Whitlam as Prime Minister after the opposition party
leaders had threatened to use their one-vote majority in the
Senate to cut off the government's supply, Elizabeth's Australia passed into what the writer Frank Moorhouse described
as a period of 'cold civil war'. This 'war' soon developed its
rituals: protesting demonstrations (usually small) against Kerr
at some of his public appearances received considerable television coverage; on the first anniversary of the sacking there
were large commemorative rallies of protest in all the main

cities. As well as being the celebration of the end of a world war of which few Australians now have any contemporary memory, the date '11 November' acquired a local mythic meaning.

For Kerr himself what may have hurt more than the demonstrations, for which he seemed to have developed a kind of confrontationist contempt, was the way the functions he attended or hosted were boycotted by Labour politicians (who governed three of the six States and many local councils) and by a large proportion of Australian intellectuals. Kerr has always enjoyed conversation with intellectuals and people in the Labour movement; in 1976 his conversation was largely confined to members of the conservative establishments.

From both sides feelings bubbled up. For instance, for the first time in its fifty years' existence the Australian Council of Trade Unions called a national strike. It was only for one day, but it was on a basically political issue and the large, if in some cases grudging, turnout of blue-collar unionists and, even more, the readiness of so many diverse factions of union leaders to agree on such a move, were seen as a sign of the alienation produced at least among the activists by last year's crisis. Policy attitudes tested in opinion polls showed a sharper than usual polarization. Overseas visitors could find a kind of sullen distractedness in the people they met. Perhaps most interesting of all, in an opinion poll published towards the end of 1976, 34 per cent of those interviewed said Kerr should resign; after the don't-knows and don't-cares were eliminated, only 49 per cent said positively that he should not resign, which is not much support for an office-holder who is supposed to unite the nation.

As can happen when an apparent consensus is disturbed, in Elizabeth's Australia there was anxious debate about what the rules of Australian political life were now supposed to be. The winners redefined the rules to make them even more comfortable for themselves. The losers felt rejected by the political system; at the extremity they fell into apathy or even an anger that contemplated methods outside the old rules. Feelings became particularly passionate in the ethnic communities, and were often expressed in old European antagonisms. In this context the figure of Kerr became a symbol of wider discontent. The parameters of Australian radicalism, on the right as well as the left, were disclosed. On the extreme royalist right Kerr was seen as a true Briton, who preserved Queen Elizabeth's Australian realm by sacking a corrupt government that was about to install a republican and communist dictatorship; on the far left he was a CIA agent planted by the United States imperialists and acting in the interests of the mining companies. Far-left hopes for a Maoist Australia in a Maoist south-east Asia confronted far-right ambitions for a racist, anglocentric, royalist, authoritarian Australia.

In the more moderate, and majority, areas the division became symbolized, among other unusual events, by the battle of the national anthems. During the 1975 election the conservative Liberal and National Country parties sang 'God Save the Queen' at their rallies. At the Labour party rallies (if they remembered the words) they sang 'Advance Australia Fair'. As a result of this kind of situation protests against Kerr's action can affect how people in Britain and Australia see each other. After all, 'God Save the Queen' *is* Queen Elizabeth's song, and, according to the constitution, the Governor-General *is* her representative.

As one who has said for years that the sharing of the same monarch could ultimately harm relations between Britain and Australia, I may face the embarrassment of seeing these prophecies come true. While the official preparations were being made for the Queen's visit to Australia in March 1977, protesters were planning anti-Kerr demonstrations to coincide with it. Almost inevitably the anti-Kerr movements could be seen in Britain as anti-British. There was a clash of interest between British and Australian monarchists. The British monarchists wanted the Australian Governor-Generalship kept out of politics – for instance in 1976 *The Times* urged Australia, in the interests of the monarchy, to replace Kerr with Prince Charles – but, to Australian monarchists, Kerr's resignation would seem a disastrous defeat. For the sake of their own legitimacy, they had to keep him *in* politics. Some of Kerr's opponents also wanted him to remain Governor-General, but an unpopular Governor-General, a lesson to any future Governor-General who attempted to intervene in politics.

The self-interest of both sides was involved in the demonstrations against Kerr, if for different reasons. On the one hand, the interest was in the deterrent effect of demonstrations. On the other, there were some hopes that these demonstrations would repel middle-class feeling (which in Australia is seen by many as the main mood) and rebound against the Labour party. In these calculations the Queen's visit became a highly political event. Some of the Liberals privately hoped that the anti-Kerr demonstrations then would discredit the Labour party, even though Labour party members themselves welcomed the Queen's visit; some of the Labour party people privately hoped that the demonstrations would discredit Kerr, without bouncing back on them.

Under circumstances of such bitter calculation it is difficult to believe that it was supporters of the remaining British constitutional links with Australia who suggested that Prince Charles should replace Kerr as Governor-General. That is a suggestion that might more logically have come from the republicans. Although one must add, in fairness to the republicans, that practically none of them has any personal animus towards Queen Elizabeth, nor, for that matter, towards Britain.

What has brought the British (and Australian) monarchy

directly into Australian politics is the Australian constitution. This written document is an Act of the British Parliament (which could, in theory, repeal it), but it was put together by Australian colonial politicians in the 1890s when, after a series of dealings, the six Australian colonies came together in a federation. The document they agreed on is a monarchic constitution, that is to say, it presents power as coming from the monarch, not, as would happen in a democratic constitution, from the people.

It is possible for a monarchy to have a declaredly democratic constitution – the first article of the Swedish constitution, for example, declares that 'All public power in Sweden emanates from the people', yet the constitution also says that the Swedish head of state is the King – but neither democratic aspiration nor nationalist aspiration were predominant in the dealings of those 1890s Australian politicians. They patched together their compact, knowing that it had puzzles, but they left those problems for the future – in a constitution that was particularly difficult to amend. One of the methods by which they concealed the incomplete nature of their business was by drawing up the document in the spirit of royalist flattery common in the age of Queen Victoria.

Since this document says in effect that Queen Elizabeth, as Queen Victoria's present heir, is governing Australia through her vice-regal representative, it is worth spending a few paragraphs summarizing it. In the first place, it makes no reference to the Cabinet, which is normally thought of as the government of Australia, nor does it make any reference to the Prime Minister. What it says is that 'the executive power' of Australia, which is to say the governing of Australia, is vested in the Queen, but it can be delegated to a Governor-General, as the Queen's representative.

The Governor-General, according to the constitution, has a Federal Executive Council to advise him in his governing. He can appoint anyone he likes to this Council, and dismiss anyone he doesn't like. The nearest the constitution gets to parliamentary democracy is in what it says about the appointment of ministers of state, but it sounds more like a parliament of the eighteenth century, than what is thought of as parliamentary democracy now. It says the Governor-General can appoint anyone he likes as a 'Queen's Minister of State' to head a government department, but anyone so appointed must become a member of Parliament within three months. It also says the Governor-General can dismiss a minister if he wants to. To round off the Governor-General's executive powers, as a representative of the monarch, the constitution says he holds the chief command of the armed forces.

The constitution is almost as generous in what it says about the Queen's law-making powers in Australia, although she is not declared the sole legislating authority. In this respect it is more limited than the other declaration that she is the sole governing authority. The very first section of the constitution says: 'The legislative power of the Commonwealth shall be vested in a Federal Parliament, which shall consist of the Queen, a Senate, and a House of Representatives.' Section 59 goes so far as to say that the Queen may herself veto any law passed by the Australian Houses of Parliament. The Governor-General, as her representative, according to the constitution, may also veto laws passed by the Houses of Parliament; or, if he wants to, he can send recommended amendments back to them. To complete this catalogue of feudal rights, the constitution leaves it to the Governor-General to decide when it is fit for Parliament to meet, when its sittings should be suspended, and when, in the case of the Lower House, it should be dissolved and sent off to an election.

The powers attributed to the Queen directly, or to her through the Governor-General, are not 'reserve powers' of the ineffable kind spoken of in Britain. They are written down in a document, and if they are to be interpreted literally, one can say that they are quite clear. One can also say that they are quite undemocratic. However, they have usually been thought of as 'reserve' powers, but in a different sense: that they weren't to be taken literally as *duties*; that, if they were to be used at all, there would have to be some extraordinary occasion for using them.

Many Australians (including some of the framers of the constitution) simply saw them as polite nonsense, with no practical application. They assumed that the question of who was the government was decided, as it normally is in parliamentary democracies, by Parliament, or, if there were two Houses of Parliament, by the more popularly elected house – in Australia's case, the House of Representatives – and that the function of the Governor-General was simply a function of ceremony, so far as public occasions were concerned, although he might have two private rights: the right to know what was going on, and the right to provide advice to members of the government if he felt like it.

Such views have now become a matter of great contention: the only point I am making is that this is what many Australians assumed to be the practice, and they were thrown into a state of shock when it didn't come out that way.

The crisis began in the Senate, a body of undemocratic composition in the sense that it is elected on a state by state basis, with the smallest state, Tasmania, with a population of little more than 400,000 electing as many senators as New South Wales, with a population of nearly 5 million. During the three years of the Whitlam government the Senate, which was controlled by the opposition parties, blocked more legislation than had been blocked by previous Senates in the other seventy-two years of the federation. Eighteen months after Whitlam came to power the Senate threatened to withhold supply; Whitlam accepted the challenge and called an election, in which he won a majority of votes and retained control of the Lower House but, because of the voting system, did not gain a majority in the Senate. A little over a year later the opposition parties again used their control of the Senate to threaten the government, by deferring the passing of supply, this time catching it in a period of greater unpopularity or, as Malcolm Fraser put it, 'with its pants down'.

This time Whitlam decided to 'tough it out'. He seemed ready to risk waiting until the economic results of the Senate's actions were obvious enough to voters for them to vote the old Senate out, because of its actions. This was a tactic that had been twice used in disputes between the two Houses of the Victorian Parliament in the nineteenth century. But this time it was not allowed to be used. Before supply ran out, and therefore before the will of the opposition senators had really been tested, and at a time that gave the opposition rather than Whitlam a political advantage, Kerr sacked Whitlam (he had given no previous indication of this intention), appointed Malcolm Fraser 'caretaker' Prime Minister, dissolved Parliament and called an election. Because of the basis of Senate elections, one result of this action was that the opposition parties have been virtually guaranteed control of the Senate for two normal lifetimes of the House of Representatives, so that, even if Labour won the 1978 election, it would still face a hostile Senate, which might be prepared to repeat the whole process all over again. If Prince Charles became Governor-General, he would inherit this situation.

If knowing what to do is just a question of looking up the written constitution, Kerr clearly had the power to sack all his ministers, appoint new ministers, dissolve Parliament and call an election. But he also argued that it was his 'constitutional duty' to act as he did. When asked about this at a National Press Club luncheon six months later, the Chief Justice, who had also used this phrase, admitted that there was no section of the written constitution that laid it down as the duty of the Governor-General to act as Kerr did: instead he put up questions of convention (which is a different matter) and of efficient government (which seems an unusual matter for an appointed official to concern himself with, since this is usually seen as the duty of elected persons).

So Australia has three problems: the consensus is fractured; the Senate is believed by many to have been strengthened as a weapon to use against future Labour governments; and many Australians now see the Governor-General as both public guardian and unique interpreter of the constitution, and they believe that the constitution itself expressly covered the situation Kerr found himself in. The fact that it doesn't has been overcome by some conservative politicians and lawyers by simple assertion: they just say it does. Along with the Senate, the Governor-General is seen as representing the true interests of the nation. It is with such highly conservative doctrines that Queen Elizabeth, as Queen of Australia, necessarily becomes associated, even if only in name.

The Queen of course has nothing to do with it. If the constitution were to be interpreted literally, she could appoint or dismiss Governors-General at will and, subject to the constitution, define their powers, but there is no likelihood of her acting in this way. To those Australians who write to Buckingham Palace asking her to sack Kerr her secretaries regularly reply to the effect that it would not be proper for her to intervene in matters that are within the jurisdiction of the Governor-General, that her only constitutional function in relation to Australia is to appoint or dismiss Governors-General on the recommendation of Australian Prime Ministers.

One such letter I have seen reads like this:

I am commanded by the Queen to acknowledge your message about the political situation in Australia.

The Australian Constitution (written by Australians, and which can only be changed by Australians) gives to the Governor-General (who is appointed by the Queen on the advice of her

Australian Prime Minister) certain very specific constitutional functions and responsibilities.

The written constitution, and accepted constitutional conventions, preclude The Queen from intervening personally in those functions once the Governor-General has been appointed, or from interfering with His Excellency's tenure of office except upon advice from the Australian Prime Minister.

It's not as simple as that. For a minority of Australians the Queen's refusal to act last year became part of their litany of protest. But there is an even greater complication, which is that, although the Governor-General is, by Queen Elizabeth's own definition of the matter, merely an official appointed by the Prime Minister, for those who care for it he nevertheless still carries the prestige of the British monarchy.

I suggested in my book *Death of the Lucky Country* that on 11 November Australia entered into the period of 'the Governor-Generalate'. In the Governor-Generalate an official appointed by the Prime Minister is seen by many Australians as monarch, still shining with the glamour and authority of the English Crown; he is also seen as chief judge or delphic oracle, unique interpreter of a constitution that is to be taken literally, and he is seen as chief politician and principal guardian of the national interest, a person whose political judgement is taken to be superior to that of elected persons. But as monarch-judge-politician a Governor-General suffers none of the checks that normally apply to monarchs, judges and politicians. As chief politician he is not accountable, not even subject to questioning; as chief judge he is not subject to such checks as public hearings, adversary argument or the need for majority agreement among fellow judges; and as monarch he is not subject to the same checks as Queen Elizabeth. I am sure that Queen Elizabeth has a sense of the democratic decencies, but even if she didn't her actions are restrained by the knowledge that, if she makes one serious mistake, she might sacrifice her whole dynasty. An Australian

Governor-General, if he loses, simply goes out on a good pension.

It is in its relations with 'the Governor-Generalate' that the future of the British monarchy may lie in Australia. In this context Australia's constitutional link with Britain becomes a stock theme in media questioning. The word 'republic' must have occurred in the newspapers more often in 1976 than in the whole of the previous ten years. Thus in November Kerr assures an audience in South Australia that Australia will still be a constitutional monarchy in a hundred years; then before an audience in Melbourne he dimisses mention of a republic as 'a little loose talk', merely 'a floating notion'; but in the same month in a television interview Whitlam says that the monarchy is no longer a symbol of unity in Australia but of division and that Australia will become a republic within the lifetime of his children. While at the 11 November rallies most of those present raise their hands in support of a republic, the Premier of Queensland announces that he has sent one of his law officers to England to develop ways of ensuring that the State of Queensland will remain a monarchy.

When Fraser replaced Whitlam, they started painting the royal crests back on to the letterboxes. 'Imperial honours' were strengthened by again awarding knighthoods. (Along with New Zealand, Papua-New Guinea, Fiji, Mauritius, the Bahamas, Grenada and Britain itself, Australia still preserves the Order of the British Empire.) Knighthoods were added to the Order of Australia that Whitlam had established, thereby prompting Patrick White, the Nobel Prize-winning novelist, and Dr H. C. Coombs, formerly Governor of the Reserve Bank, to resign from the Order. A union leader who accepted one of Fraser's knighthoods was ostracized by unionists and Labour politicians. A Labour appointee to the High Court refused a knighthood. By actions such as these some of the symbols of the British connection become symbols of the conservative political parties in Australia.

What other symbols remain? 'God Save the Queen' is played as a national anthem at some conservative functions; at other functions there is a choice between the three tunes designated as national songs (Malcolm Fraser prefers 'Waltzing Matilda') or nothing at all. The top left-hand quarter of the Australian flag still contains the Union Jack. The state governors (almost beyond belief) are still, officially, representatives of the British government and from their Rolls Royces, or the flagpoles of their government houses they fly the Union Jack rather than the national or state flag. In certain kinds of legal cases there can still be appeals to the Privy Council in London and reference can still be made in the law courts to the idea of 'imperial law'. In theory the constitutional basis of all seven of the Australian governments lies in Britain. In all seven governments the fiction is maintained that an entity referred to as 'the Crown' is the government.

In public opinion surveys a majority of those interviewed say they want Australia to remain a monarchy. There would seem to be little doubt that Queen Elizabeth herself is still popular; even by those who don't take to celebrity worship she would at least be seen as hard-working and well-meaning. For some of those who want Australia to remain a monarchy the attraction may be in the monarchic idea itself; for others the preservation of 'Britishness' can be seen as most significant; for others it may be more a matter of preferring the system you know to the system you don't; other support seems to come more than anything else from apathy.

According to the exact nature of the questions asked, and the mood at the time, declared support in opinion polls for an Australian republic has varied between 25 per cent and 39 per cent. Over the last few years it would average at something like one person in three. Immigrants from places other than Britain show a greater than average republican tendency, and the young tend to be more republican than the old. To people like myself who believe Australia should have its own head of state (although not, I would hope, with the feudal powers of the Governor-General) the public opinion polls show a pleasing potential. Since there has been no sustained campaign for a republic, it seems remarkable that, without a campaign, support has already drifted to somewhere around one in three Australians, or at least one in four, and that there are a large number of don't-knows or don't cares. This suggests that, when the time comes, support would grow quickly. I would guess that the professed monarchists, the really hard-liners, the over-my-dead-body brigade, may be as little as one in five, one in four, something like that.

When will the time come? The usual reply of Labour leaders – who don't want to offend the monarchists – is that the republic will come, but not in their lifetime. When I'm asked the question, I say that it could come within ten years. It's a wild guess, but it's intended to suggest that it is later than people think.

The essential point to understand is that, whatever preferences people may have for either monarchies or republics, the real question in Australia is not the monarchy–republic question but that of national identity involved in Australia having its own head of state. If Australians had their own royal family, as the Scandinavian countries and the Low Countries do, it might not seem worth the effort to do anything more than democratize them and photograph them riding bicycles. But Australia's monarch lives 12,000 miles away, in London, and is primarily the head of state of a nation that is not Australia.

This distant nation is one with which many of the old bonds have gone – most obviously the bonds of money and guns. Earlier Britain was overwhelmingly important as Australia's main trading partner; now it can't even hold the third place it slipped to after it was superseded by Japan and the United States. And, while some Australians may still live so nostalgically that they can imagine that Britain might still be of strategic significance to Australia (in a university debate I spoke at in 1976 one conservative politician brought the house down when he said that in some future emergency Australia could 'shelter under Britain's nuclear umbrella'), most Australians have now emerged into reality sufficiently to understand that Britain is no longer of military significance to them. Most would see the United States as their military guarantor; others might seek alliances in Asia; some would prefer an independent Australian policy.

There was a period when more people living in Australia may have referred to themselves as 'British' than as 'Australian'. That period has gone. But not only has 'Australian' replaced 'British'; the word 'ethnic' has come, to emphasize the diversity of Australians' national origins. When the Sydney magazine the *Bulletin* ran a series on ethnic groups in Australia, I heard criticism that they hadn't included the English as an ethnic group. While until the end of the Second World War immigration was overwhelmingly British, something like a third of immigrants in Australia now are not British, and about a fifth of all Australians are immigrants. To some of the 'ethnics' the monarchy can be both an ideological insult (they believe in republicanism) and a national insult (as continental Europeans they do not wish to pay even token allegiance to an Englishwoman).

But the greatest ground swell will prove to be among the native born, with their new perceptions of national consciousness, reflected not only in terms of trade and military strategy, but in general views of the world. There is now a much greater self-confidence in the arts and in intellectual life: the typical Australian intellectual is no longer an expatriate living in London, or wishing to live in London. Even those Australians who find Australian life flat and unimportant are as likely to look to other world centres for relief as to Britain. And there is increasing recognition of Australia's geographic position, as a large island between the Indian and Pacific Oceans, adjoining the archipelago of south-east Asia and the small island-nations of the south-west Pacific. While his Liberal party predecessors would always make their first symbolic overseas visits to Washington and London, Malcolm Fraser's first important overseas trips were to Tokyo and Washington.

To the domestic drifts towards more confident national self-definition one can add the external factor that, of the three nations (Britain, Canada, New Zealand) with whom the sharing of a monarch can seem significant to Australians, Britain is faced with a civil war in Northern Ireland and a separatist movement in Scotland, and Canada has Quebec. With such possibilities of turmoil in heartlands of Anglo-Saxondom 'the Crown' can no longer seem the inevitably binding force it may have appeared when such a large part of the world map was coloured red. To these intimations of the possible disintegration of Britain and Canada are added, in Australia itself, the new views of 'the Crown' (viz. the Governor-General) as a cause of national disunity.

Perhaps what is remarkable about Australia is not that a discussion is now going on about how, like almost every other nation on earth, Australia might have its own head of state, but that the discussion should have taken so long to begin.

ELIZABETH LONGFORD

Personal Styles in Twentieth-Century Monarchy

IN a controversial letter to *The Times* of November 1976 Sir Con O'Neill, a distinguished retired diplomat, called on Britain to 'modernize'. We should abolish such traditional flummeries, he wrote, as mayoral robes and chain, legal wigs, and titles like Sir (including Sir Con) and Esquire. But, when Mr Con turned to the lady who had conferred his 'ridiculous' knighthood upon him, he changed his tune: 'I except the monarchy from these strictures,' he wrote. 'Today it is the most efficient and the most popular of our institutions, and if you have a monarchy it must have style.'

Yes, but what style? Who could have believed that the gay, impetuous style of the young Queen Victoria would ever change into the secluded mystery of the Widow at Windsor? The Monarch could fairly have been called a recluse for years, a fact which caused a slight rise in republican temperatures. True, she made some out-going gestures (not approved by her family) by publishing the best-selling *Leaves* from her Highland journal followed by *More Leaves* (and more disapproval). In Scotland she always remained the Monarch of the Glen, not of the closet. The British veneration for age together with Victoria's strongly held views on the solemnity of her office (she was caught smiling only twice in photographs) combined to develop a mystique, almost a mortal terror, of majesty. Even her own household would flee in

45

panic if caught by her unawares, crying 'The Queen! the Queen!' To Sir Harold Nicolson, as an Eton boy, she looked like a Chinese idol, only half human and infinitely remote. When she died in 1901, the monarchy might have withdrawn for ever into a golden but impenetrable mist; visibility nil.

King Edward VII had not been initiated while Prince of Wales into the duties of heir. His mother considered him too indiscreet. So he had turned to another arena – pleasure. His accession meant that the opportunities for display were multiplied. The fashionable dresses of his beautiful Danish wife Alexandra had always contrasted startlingly with her mother-in-law's well-worn wardrobe. Mr Gladstone's great-niece suspected that the old Queen had not ordered a new outfit even for her Diamond Jubilee. 'Can it have been the same bonnet and mantle that she wore ten years before? Well, it looked like it.' Queen Alexandra's clothes always looked newer than new.

Hitherto the secrecy of Edward's adventures with Skittles, the little equestrian courtesan from Liverpool, or with the Parisian Cora Pearl, covered only by a sprig of parsley, had depended on the tact of a discreet Press. His prodigious gambling exploits had not fully caught the public eye. W. S. Blunt, the diarist, heard from his friend Skittles that HRH had actually played baccarat in a room behind the Court Room, during the notorious Baccarat Case. 'What if the public had found out?' But the Press did not split. Now, in 1901, the King could really let himself go in more public and constructive ways. Pageantry was again part of the royal style.

Lord Esher, an expert on pageantry, who had staged Queen Victoria's Diamond Jubilee, realized that public celebrations could plunge at a stroke from grandeur into fiasco. King Edward VII's splendid Coronation was by no means free from contretemps. One Baronet had a fit in the Abbey, one peeress temporarily lost her coronet down a lavatory, the Archbishop lost his place, the Queen got a drop of the sacred oil on her nose, which was not allowed to twitch on any account, a Duchess tripped up and rolled over to the feet of a Cabinet minister, and Lord Esher himself created a Guy Fawkes-type alarm by popping off champagne corks in the vaults after the ceremony was over. Though the new King was no great reader, he may have known that at his mother's Coronation Lord Rolle had also taken a toss, while several peers had quaffed champagne at a side altar. *Plus ça change ...*

On wider issues he exchanged his mother's extensive desk work for chats with any ministers he happened to come across, favoured France rather than Germany (despite his ancestry and guttural *rs*) and assisted at the rebirth of the *Entente Cordiale*. In this he moved away from his mother's bellicose style ('Oh, if the Queen were a man, she would like to go and give those Russians ... such a beating!') towards his father's belief in 'international reciprocity'. A contemporary, Harold Begbie, neatly expressed the new style in a parody of *Struwwelpeter* (1901):

> Babies, when you leave the pram
> Do not emulate Lord Pam:
> English bluffness always quench,
> Learn to speak Parisian French;
> If it do not make you shine,
> It will help you, dears, to dine.

The King was a convivial diner-out, with his subjects and also with Americans, wreathing himself in cigar smoke and generous dreams of universal happiness. Unlike his mother he greatly enjoyed the company of his heir. As for continuity, it showed in Edward VII's powerful sense of public decorum, expressed among other things in regal punctuality. All told, his short reign of one decade had humanized the monarchy at a time when the human touch was needed.

With King George V's accession four years before the out-break of the First World War, the monarchy took another step forward on the road to democratization. But not really because of anything the King might wish. On the contrary, George V was temperamentally more conservative than either his father or grandmother. The changes came from outside. From the war itself.

The new King's character was not a subtle one. Intensely upright, honest and straightforward, most of his idiosyn-crasies had been nurtured in the Royal Navy, and included a loud quarter-deck manner and devotion to discipline. The new generation might be warned against 'English bluffness', but the English King made no attempt to 'quench' it in himself. He was deeply attached to his wife, the shy and stately Queen Mary, but found it impossible to form a close relationship with any of his children, especially the heir. 'I was always frightened of my father,' he would say, 'they must be fright-ened of me.' In this respect his royal style towards the heir had reverted to the bad old English tradition of the eighteenth and nineteenth centuries. Nevertheless a perceptive observer like Esher could be impressed by the quiet domesticity of King George's Court, hopefully predicting a return to the style of Queen Victoria.

In other ways the new Court was inferior to its predecessor. George V was rather more philistine about the arts than Edward VII, neither boasting like his father that he under-stood artistic 'ar-r-r-angement', nor giving his intelligent wife, Queen Mary, much encouragement to develop her artistic instincts in the public sphere. She patronized needlework and became a voracious private collector. The King's own work in these directions was reserved for his remarkable royal stamp collection at Buckingham Palace, and for the needling and pin-pricking of 'David' (Prince of Wales, and later King Edward VIII) about his unorthodox suits and shoes. The King obstinately rejected criticisms that his Court was unnecessarily stiff. Had he not visited Continental Courts in his youth and seen real pomposity at work? To wear a ribbon or star even a centimetre out of line was as bad, he considered, as if a man let his shirt hang outside his trousers.

With the outbreak of war all the King's true and strong qualities came to the fore. If he always remained critical of youth (short skirts, bobbed hair, cigarettes and bottle parties), he now showed the extent of self-sacrifice which his own standards imposed. He consented to change the name of the royal House from the German Coburg to the English Windsor, though any form of chauvinism went much against the grain. He bore with fortitude a severe accident at the front, when his horse threw him. He even accepted the suggestion of Lloyd George, his Prime Minister, that the Court should be teetotal, as an example to the allegedly drunken munition workers. The House of Commons did not follow his lead. But Lloyd George, who had derided 'the peacocking of royalty' in his youth (a hit at King Edward VII), could not use such words of King George V.

No one ever supposed that the King approved of all, or indeed of any, typically post-war innovations: the 'un-English' habit of week-ending; Labour governments; women MPs; the 'flapper' vote; Mahatma Gandhi's bare knees at Buckingham Palace; or the slow but sure movement of his realms overseas towards independence. But his public face was perfect. He made the new Labour ministers feel at home; and as a reward Mr 'Jimmy' Thomas made HM feel at home – in an atmosphere of affection expressed in the welcome words, 'Has your Majesty heard this one?' Mr Attlee was also to reward the King with a telling note of approval: as a profoundly constitutional monarch he had become 'a rallying point of stability' in a rapidly changing world, and a focus for 'sympathy with new ideas'. If the King-Emperor himself could dutifully receive the members of a *socialist* ministry, others must also make the effort to understand the new era into which they all, high and low, had been born.

George V presented his subjects with a splendid innovation of his own. His messages on the radio, broadcast in a resonant but completely natural voice, brought him closer to the people than any other act, including appearances on the famous balcony of Buckingham Palace. His last message was delivered movingly at his Silver Jubilee to his 'very very dear people'. To his surprise and humble joy, he also had become 'very dear' to them.

It is not easy to pin a 'style of monarchy' to Edward VIII. He succeeded in January 1936 and signed his Abdication papers that December. At least a quarter of his evanescent reign had lain under the shadow of that rare and romantic event. For Edward VIII alone of English Sovereigns voluntarily surrendered the throne – and surrendered it for love.

Perhaps the best one can do is to construct a kingly style for him, based partly on his apprenticeship as Prince of Wales, partly on his eleven-month reign and partly also on what *might* have happened if he had worn the crown until his death in 1972.

His outstanding qualities as Prince of Wales were quickly recognized by a nation prepared to idolize this yellow-haired, blue-eyed charmer, who was always smiling: brave like all his house, either during the First World War or on the hunting field; addicted to strenuous exercise, to walking rather than being driven, and inclined to telephone rather than send a royal messenger; friendly and out-going when abroad, a born communicator; generously concerned about suffering, especially that of the unemployed, among whom he was to move as King with a special imaginative sympathy and grace; violently allergic to all stuffiness, and fired, apparently, with a crusading spirit to carry the monarchy, if possible without too much kicking and screaming from the household, into the mid-twentieth century. When his father's courtier, Sir Frederick Ponsonby, insisted that the monarchy should remain on a pedestal in order to retain its mystery and influence, the Prince silenced him with the words, 'Times are changing'. His future historical label seemed ready and waiting to be affixed: 'Edward the Modernizer'.

What his supporters could not see was that a permanent immaturity of mind and heart had caused their hero to be fatally flawed. When he loved, he loved 'abjectly', writes his biographer Frances Donaldson, nor was he capable of falling in love except with married women, of whom the twice-married and divorced Mrs Simpson was to become his grand passion. Moreover his biographer found in him no real understanding either of national or personal problems. 'Both at the time of the Abdication and for the rest of his life', she writes, 'the King would always show the most extraordinary obtuseness in relation to the facts.'

One fact that cannot be ignored is the contrast between Edward's fertile ambitions as a royal modernizer and his almost barren achievement. He himself conceded that his only practical reforms were to make beefeaters' beards optional and to establish the King's Flight. (One might add a tendency to demote the hat. He was the first monarch to step from a plane bare-headed, and whenever he did wear a hat it was always tilted, as if he would like it to fly off.) Nor is there evidence of any substantial break-through in an anti-snobbish, democratic or any other sense after he was freed from the trammels of monarchy and living with his wife in Paris. He insisted on referring to his Duchess as Her Royal Highness, though in youth he had affected to despise all meaningless 'pomp and ritual'. His Investiture robes, for instance, he had called 'a preposterous rig'.

His youthful rebellion against authority was not reforming zeal but merely the anger of a thwarted schoolboy, for which the harsh 'naval' discipline of his father and the repressions of his mother must be held partly responsible. Eventually his best qualities were to shine out, not as those of a 'modern' King, but as an old-fashioned romantic lover. From this latter ideal he never deviated an inch, his 'style' emerging as one of utter loyalty, devotion and self-sacrifice – to his fair lady. He might have been a knight from some remote age of chivalry.

From all this one thing seems clear. King Edward VIII under no circumstances would have left his mark as a genuinely 'modernizing' monarch. His wife was far too clever to have tried 'Americanizing' the English Court, and he himself was not clever enough to translate those vague feelings of rebellion, characteristic of youth the world over, into a new system. No doubt he would have abolished some of the ceremonial, leaving himself more time for – what? One is tempted to answer, perhaps over-cynically, for more trips to the Mediterranean.

King George VI's personal style was little short of heroic. This will not sound so exaggerated to those who have read about the baby tortured by gastric attacks, the left-handed child made to use his right, with legs in splints, and burdened by an appalling stammer, the tendency to fail exams and the eclipsing older brother. As a young man, the disastrous tides continued to beat against King George V's second son. His naval career during the First World War was almost wrecked by an undiagnosed duodenal ulcer, though by sheer will-power he did manage to fight in the battle of Jutland. After the ulcer was diagnosed and operated upon, the Prince had to resign from his chosen service, the Navy. He took up flying – not a congenial pursuit, though it made him the first King of England to be a fully qualified pilot. It was also valuable to have commanded cadets at Cranwell who would later become cogs in the industrial machine. This gave the Prince a permanent sympathy with the nation's youth. Another consolation was to be created Duke of York by his father, which in turn produced self-confidence and a sudden inspiration – 'Let's have a camp'. The annual Duke of York's Camps, with their sports and their sing-songs, were his most characteristic contribution over many years, showing as they did the man's practical idealism and modest resolve to mix with ordinary people 'under the spreading chestnut tree' of social service.

Despite everything, moreover, there had been enough happiness in his childhood at Sandringham to build upon later, when things at last began to go right. His cousin, Prince Louis Mountbatten, had been up with him at Cambridge, and this enduring friendship was to stand him in good stead when what seemed to him the greatest disaster of all struck. Meanwhile he played championship tennis and fell in love with and proposed to the entrancing Lady Elizabeth Bowes-Lyon. Blissfully happy in her own large family, however, with romantic homes in Scotland and Hertfordshire, and a house in London, this twenty-year-old girl saw no reason to exchange her freedom for the constricting if magical circle of royalty. Was that to be the Duke's ultimate frustration?

Fortunately the setbacks of his youth had taught him never to give up. He pursued 'the most marvellous person in the World' for nearly two years, and at length was able to send his mother a triumphant telegram, 'Alright. Bertie' – Bertie being his name in the family. They married in 1923.

Domestic serenity was highlighted by the birth of his two daughters, Elizabeth and Margaret, and by the discovery of a speech therapist (Lionel Logue) who taught him to control his stammer. His Commonwealth tour was particularly enjoyable because of the universal enthusiasm that the Duchess's charm won for them both. 'Why, they're human,' a New Zealander had gasped, after the Duchess waved back and smiled 'right into my face'.

In 1930 there seemed a chance that the Duke might go to Canada as Governor-General. 'Jimmy' Thomas, however, decided against it: 'They did not want a Royalty in Canada.'

No one, least of all the Duke himself, saw in this reticent member of the royal family the future King.

If Edward VIII had been the Uncrowned King, George VI began his reign as the Unknown King. He was forty-one at his accession but had never been trained for kingship, nor was he really sure of his brother's intentions until a few weeks before the Abdication. He confessed that he 'sobbed like a child' at the awful prospect, and his own supposed inadequacy. He suffered from shock. 'Dickie, this is absolutely terrible,' he groaned to his cousin, Lord Louis Mountbatten, 'I'm quite unprepared for it ... I've never even seen a State Paper. I'm only a Naval Officer, it's the only thing I know about.' Dickie Mountbatten came up with a miraculous reply. ' "There is no finer training for a king." ' He was quoting the words of his father, Prince Louis of Battenberg, to *his* cousin, the future George V, when *his* elder brother passed the succession to him by dying suddenly in 1892. Notwithstanding this genuine encouragement, George VI's self-distrust was to remain, especially when he had to broadcast. His stammer had been virtually cured, but not the long pauses before alarming letters like *c* in constitution. Many public men felt that the Abdication would shake the monarchy to its foundations and perhaps topple it. Was poor George VI the man to salvage such a wreck, they asked themselves. Sir Henry ('Chips') Channon the diarist and close friend of the Windsors described the new monarch as utterly unimpressive, devoid of 'thrill' and totally lacking in 'the divinity that doth hedge a king'.

Family solidarity and a wave of popular feeling for the man who had stepped into the breach supported the King during the first months of strain. Then he showed his mettle.

King George VI was to rule with a style of his own, despite the view of his brother 'David' that 'Bertie' was their father all over again. No doubt father and son both loved familiar places and people. But, whereas George V's geniality consisted in rough 'chaffing' – a masculine approach which was meant to be funny but could be hurtful – King George VI possessed both extreme sensitivity and salty wit. The elegantly balanced 'Skylon', for instance, which graced the Festival of Britain he described as an unfortunate symbol for the British economy, since it had 'no visible means of support'. On one occasion Sir Charles Russell, QC, was inadvertently presented to him twice over, first correctly as Chancellor of the Duchy of Lancaster, then incorrectly as Chancellor of the Duchy of Cornwall. The King realized the mistake but merely remarked, 'You seem to be in considerable demand'.

His inexperience of state papers made him appreciate all ministers who took him into their confidence. Chamberlain, Churchill and Bevin won his special gratitude and tributes like: 'Bevin is very good & tells me everything that is going on.'

Throughout the Second World War people found in him and his Queen, unlike the 'Skylon', their visible means of moral support. He became a personal intermediary particularly with the Americans. The bombing of Buckingham Palace, though it jangled his nerves, drew him closer to the people of Coventry and London who had suffered more than he. When D Day came, both he and Churchill proposed to sail with the fleet. Rather than land the country with a possible change of Sovereign and Premier at the same moment, they struck a bargain of mutual abstention.

Notwithstanding the King's spirit, the war bruised a temperament which, though steadfast, was easily depressed. 'I feel burnt out,' he wrote afterwards, and Attlee pronounced him 'rather a worrying type'. His personal courage in face of increasing ill-health gave the last years of his reign a pathos which the people did not fail to appreciate. He looked so young yet so worn.

A reign dedicated to stabilizing the country and throne

could never stand out in high relief. But, if George VI's style was unobtrusive, it bore the hallmark of sincerity. His father had been an expert detector of anything that he considered 'un-English'. The son was a model of what most Englishmen would like to be: athletic, quietly amusing, ready to learn, modest and selfless.

Lady Astor once congratulated Edward VIII on his modern style of royalty. 'It will make things easier,' she said, 'for your successor.'

That last prediction turned out to be wildly ironic. Far from easing George VI's task, the Abdication caused a jolt that made 'modern monarchies' or 'new styles' seem almost indecent. But, with time and the healing influence of George VI and his wife, the royal equilibrium returned. When Queen Elizabeth II came to the throne on 6 February 1952, the country was ready for a fresh start. And there is little doubt that Edward VIII's experiments in 'modern monarchy', however inconclusive, were to make things easier for his niece.

For her the process did not come without effort. She learned the hard way by trial and error, suffering at first from a sense of personal inadequacy perhaps inherited from her father, but buoyed up by unshakable faith in her office.

The emergence of the new royal 'style' has passed through various phases. Each bears the imprint of the Queen's own individuality, while at the same time there is the broad movement of a democratic monarchy to keep pace with changes in public moods, tastes and opinions. This 'satellite' movement, so to speak, has since the days of Edward VII never halted, though circumstances may change its speed. Even a temperamentally hidebound monarch like George V gave permission for his cousin Princess Marie Louise to travel by bus. Though not without the grave reflection, 'What would Grandmama have thought?' King George VI, while mildly conservative by nature, had admitted to his daughter Princess Elizabeth that in wartime a lady-in-waiting could not bicycle in a hat if she did not possess a hat.

In its satellite journey around public opinion, the 'new Elizabethan' monarchy has been inspired by the Queen but powered and quickened by the royal family as a whole. Prince Philip's landing in a helicopter at the palace at the time of the Coronation was more significant than Edward VIII's landing at Heathrow at his accession without a hat; Prince Charles's parachuting from a supersonic aircraft into the ocean, Princess Anne's insistence on going to boarding school, Prince Andrew's solo gliding, and Prince Edward's public fortitude on the royal family film, when his eldest brother's cello string snapped in his face – all these things may be straws, but they are straws in a wind of change.

What of the Queen's personal contribution? Our 'modern monarchy' is sometimes assumed to be entirely the work of that human dynamo her husband. Nothing could be more untrue. The famous modernization of Buckingham Palace, when Prince Philip began by inspecting some 600 rooms and ended by installing an intercom, was the joint enterprise of husband and wife. Extremely practical herself, with a probing interest in how things are run and a passion for good order, the Queen would be the last person to put up with inefficiency – however hallowed by tradition.

The change from 'Presentation Parties' for débutantes to small luncheons and dinners for people of all professions is one that the Queen would particularly have welcomed. She has always preferred real personal relations in a smaller context to the ritual of mass entertainment. Nevertheless some aspects of her new life proved a strain to the shy young Queen. Broadcasting Christmas messages to the Commonwealth was by now an integral part of twentieth-century style. Her father had not shirked it despite his being unable to enjoy the family Christmas until the ordeal was over. His daughter was not the one to fail, particularly as the Commonwealth was her special pride and joy. But a naturally light voice, rendered lighter by youth and nervousness, together with a touching belief that the Sovereign's manner must be weighty, the royal face serious and the royal speech somewhat archaic, produced an impression of stiltedness which the Queen, of all people, least deserved. Fortunately her profound sincerity, honesty and humility, backed by growing experience and practice, overcame these early trials. The introduction of television in the late fifties seemed at first only an added strain, involving new techniques to be mastered. Television, however, could so obviously become an invaluable adjunct to the Queen's new style, especially in its immediacy, direct contact and total personal involvement of voice, appearance, movement and general ambience, that master it she did.

Politically the fifties were a drag on any coherent style of monarchy, owing to the contradictory impulses which stirred people during these years. The Festival of Britain had opened in 1951, nine months before Elizabeth II's accession. It was to be 'A Tonic to the Nation'. The new Queen's accession was widely expected to act as a second tonic. Winston Churchill her first Prime Minister spoke of the Coronation as 'a dash of colour on our hard road'. Others, however, felt that the tonic and colour were equally misplaced: that people were less likely to reach Churchill's 'sunlit uplands' if they kept on stopping by the road-side to gawp at 'braying pageantry'. When the euphoria created by 'a new Elizabethan age' subsided, the monarchy itself appeared to fall flat.

To these problems were added several personal ones: notably the Duke of Edinburgh's role. What part was this creative and forthright young man to play in the new set-up? There was now a palace staffed by efficient secretaries to serve the Queen and no obvious niche for him beyond that of 'the Queen's husband'. Moreover even that aspect of his role had been diminished. In 1952 political pressures were exerted, it was said, upon the Queen to remove the name of Mountbatten from her House and family's style and title. The royal children were henceforth to be called Windsor.

The Duke found a valuable outlet for his energies in Commonwealth travel and conservation, sending a moving message home to his wife and family at Christmas: 'The Lord watch between thee and me . . .' But it was the Press, or a section of it, who were watching. A royal rift was reported and promptly denied by the Queen's Press Secretary. From then on Prince Philip made no bones about *his* style of royalty. He would tolerate no snooping. He would call a spade a spade, or rather, he would call a long lens poking through the royal keyhole by some name as well-merited as it was unprintable. He would, in fact, be 'bloody nasty'.

With the sixties the royal family suddenly took off. Though the Commonwealth was bursting out all over with republics, this did not deter the Queen from answering innumerable calls for visits, state and otherwise. Her insistence on flying to Ghana, despite alarmist reports of possible bombs, would remind historians of her grandfather George V's visit to Belfast in 1921 – a journey also considered ill-advised but which did great good. As regards courage, the style of the British monarchy never changes.

After Ghana, there was no question but that the Queen would again fly to Canada, separatist demos or no. It was her duty, she knew, to be the cement holding in place the Canadian mosaic and linking together the ethnic variety of the country, as well as linking Canada with the rest of the Commonwealth. Her tours of the Caribbean, Africa, Australia or India supplied for her some of the colour which the self-styled 'Affluent Society' was still enjoying at home. But for her it was not all jacaranda and frangipani. The Queen visited a leper colony in order to drive out by royal example the corroding fear of infection.

On the family front a new era dawned. Since 1957 Prince

Charles had been at school, the first heir to the throne to do this. His parents wished him and all their family to learn teamwork with other children, rather than to consider themselves 'special', in solo confrontation with governess or tutor. This procedure in Princess Elizabeth's case had not made her feel 'special' in any conceited sense – far from it – but it had seemed to set her apart, creating reserve and anxiety. Her father used to refer to her 'fretwork'.

In the sixties Prince Charles went to Gordonstoun, the 'progressive' Scottish school which had caused some raised eyebrows among Princess Elizabeth's older relations when they heard she was engaged to be married to a product of this 'crank' establishment. A generation later it had been taken for granted that the royal princes would follow their father. Moreover, with the birth of Prince Andrew, the name of Mountbatten re-entered the family tree, through the Queen's heartfelt desire and royal warrant. Though the royal house remains Windsor, when Princess Anne married in 1973, the registrar entered her surname as Mountbatten-Windsor. When the Prince of Wales marries, he will appear as Charles Mountbatten-Windsor.

All these changes indicate a more marked pattern of commonsense, normality and family cohesion. Indeed it is the partnership of the Queen and her husband which today gives its characteristic flavour to their reign. They are complementary to each other. From Prince Philip the enterprise, the thrust, the encouragement of success in national life, whether by awards, example or speeches. Sometimes the phrases are so lapidary as to cut the Prince's own fingers. But his come-back is always effective. Having been chided for criticizing the welfare state's lack of initiative in creating wealth, he replied: 'It seems to me that anything which gives people the opportunity to achieve these ambitions [to make some useful contribution to the success of their country] is an incentive – and if it happens to be legal and morally sound and not too fattening then so much the better.'

From Queen Elizabeth II the courtesy, the empathy, the gentleness, the compassion. 'If I am ever Queen,' she once said as a child, 'I shall not allow horses to work on Sundays. They need a day of rest too.' From first to last she has been kindness itself, whether it was the touchingly sincere gesture with which she pressed her first Maundy money into each outstretched hand, or the gaiety that took Richard Crossman, MP so much by surprise. 'She has a lovely laugh. She laughs with her whole face and she just can't assume a mere smile because she's really a very spontaneous person.'

King George VI used to refer to himself, his wife and their two daughters as 'the firm'. That family firm can now appeal to three generations – through the Queen and Prince Philip, their children, and the Queen Mother. The emphasis laid by the Queen on the *family* aspects both of her own Silver Wedding and of Princess Anne's non-state wedding shows how her mind is moving. Some people speak of a 'flying monarchy' because of its mobility; others of a 'working monarchy' because of its long hours with the red boxes and visitors of all kinds, from Bulganin and Khrushchev to Morecambe and Wise. Perhaps its essential style is simpler: a 'family monarchy'.

The seventies have continued to move towards relaxation and away from formality. No one in the past could have conceived of a royal family film, with shots of the Queen in slacks, or a barbecue at the Glasallt Shiel – no one, that is to say, except Queen Victoria, who built the little Glasallt after Prince Albert's death. Victoria's early passion had been for having family picnics painted by Landseer, in order to bring 'our happy home life' vividly before her subjects' eyes. If TV had been invented in her reign nothing would have stopped her appearances on it. There is much of Victoria's spontaneity in her great-great-granddaughter, not least when the Queen publicly denounces as 'obnoxious' a foreign proposal to make in this country a sick film on the sex life of Christ.

The Queen's highly successful walkabouts, both in Australia and New Zealand where they started and now in every large city she visits, again make one think of Victoria. As a shy girl, Victoria dreaded what was then called '*circléing*', that is, circulating among her guests and making conversation at each stop. The diarist Charles Greville cruelly lampooned her 'dull Court' and even duller conversational gambits. 'It was a fine day.' 'Yes, ma'am, a very fine day.' 'It was rather cold though.' 'It *was* rather cold Madam.'

Queen Elizabeth II was also a shy girl and may have felt about *circléing* much as Queen Victoria did. That the Queen now voluntarily chooses walkabouts in preference to formal presentations shows how greatly her style has relaxed with the growth of confidence and her wish to meet people.

Increasing accessibility is the key to our monarchy. One cannot imagine any other family with either the will or the training to be constantly on tap as they are. Burke's *Guide to the Monarchy* whimsically lists five Romanian Princesses among the final runners-up for the British Crown. One cannot see these ladies being invited to ascend the throne or accepting the invitation if issued. After all, Crown Princess Marie of Romania told Lady Astor she 'believed with all her heart and soul' in the Divine Right of Kings. If Britain is to be a democratic monarchy, we must have *this* royal family.

In the recent past, Sovereigns have spent up to three months of private holiday each year in the pleasure-grounds of Europe. Such a schedule would be turned down automatically by Queen Elizabeth II. For her, a lovely landscape is a Scottish landscape. Once, when a visiting potentate commented disparagingly on 'your low brown hills', the royal family were outraged. They had always thought of their heather-covered ranges as blue or purple *mountains.*

Accessibility means familiarity, a royal family with a human face, and one that is known through a whole gamut of human emotions: laughter, a quizzical smile (for a student shouting 'Queen out!' between gulps), interest, concern, boredom. Then what happens to the 'magic of monarchy' when daylight like this floods the royal scene?

The new style does not reckon on magic of the old kind. An astonishing amount of it survives notwithstanding. The Queen still meets people who lose their heads when introduced to her, like the Shakespearian actor who, when asked in what plays he had previously performed, could not remember the name of a single one.

More familiarity with the royal family, however, and less pomp and ceremony, must inevitably – and constructively – transmute the dross of magic into the gold of service. Today the Queen is deeply loved and respected because she works hard, is charming, honest, brave, humble and herself. Her attitude to pageantry is not to inflate it in times of stringency (witness her plea for moderation over her Silver Jubilee) but, when the pageantry is part of an ancient tradition, to allow the magic to work. The *Crossman Diaries* again provide insight. As Lord President, Crossman's duty was to carry the ceremonial sword of state when the Queen opened Parliament. He begged to be excused. The Duke of Norfolk, as Earl Marshal, hotly objected. Crossman therefore approached the Queen's Private Secretary, then Sir Michael Adeane. From him Crossman learned that public ceremonies could be as irksome to the Queen as to Crossman himself. 'It will certainly occur to her', continued Adeane, 'to ask herself if you should be excused when she herself has to go, since you are both officials . . . But all you need to do is to write a letter asking to be excused without stating the reason why.' Crossman did his ceremonial duty.

This episode, slight though it is, is perhaps a fitting one to end on. For it shows how much the style of monarchy has changed. Under what other Sovereign could such a dialogue have taken place? It also shows how persuasive can be reasonableness, goodness and dutifulness when they are found at the head of the state.

1. Her Majesty Queen Elizabeth II. A Coronation portrait by Cecil Beaton

2. The accession. Princess Elizabeth was in Kenya when she
became Queen on the death of her father. Here she returns
to British soil at London Airport in February 1952

3. The moment of Coronation, June 1953

4. ROYAL FAMILIES

(a) Nine Sovereigns at Windsor for the funeral of Edward VII, May 1910. (*left to right*) Haakon of Norway, Ferdinand of Bulgaria, Manuel of Portugal, Wilhelm II of Germany, George I of Greece, Albert of Belgium. (*seated*) Alfonso XIII of Spain, George V, Frederick VIII of Denmark

(b) The Queen's family at Buckingham Palace after her Coronation

5. ROYAL HOMES
(a) The blue drawing room at Buckingham Palace

(b) The east front at Windsor Castle

(c) Sandringham House, Norfolk

(d) Balmoral Castle, Aberdeenshire

6. TRAPPINGS OF MONARCHY

(a) (*left*) Peers outside the Abbey at the Coronation

(b) (*right*) Postillions and the Coronation coach

(c) (*below*) Footmen resting during the Coronation

7. THE QUEEN AS HEAD OF STATE
(a) The State Opening of Parliament, 1958

(b) The Queen at her desk, Balmoral Castle, 1972

8. WITH HER PRIME
MINISTER
(a) Sir Winston
Churchill after
dinner at 10 Downing
Street, 1955

(b) Sir Harold Wilson
at Downing Street,
1976

9. ROYAL DUTIES
(a) Trooping the
Colour, 1963

(b) A banquet
in Sâo Paulo,
Brazil, 1968

(c) With the Yeomen of the Guard, July 1974

(d) Inspecting the parade, Sovereign's Company, First Grenadier Guards, 1953

(e) New Zealand, 1970

(f) With Canadian Indian chiefs and their wives, 1976

(g) Invested as a bard, 1946

(h) Visiting Glasgow's new Fruit Market, 1969

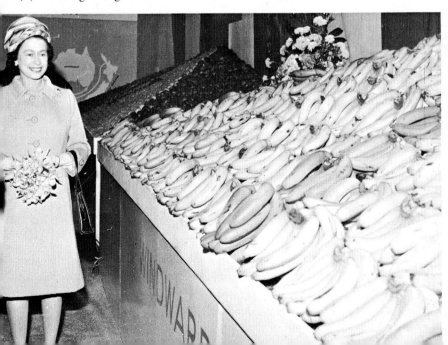

10. MEETING THE PEOPLE
(a) Aberfan after the disaster, 1966

(b) At Silverwood Colliery, South Yorkshire, 1975

(c) With the oldest Chelsea Pensioner, 1975

(d) Australia, 1970

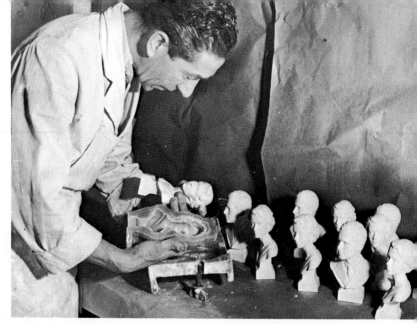

11. RESPONSES TO MONARCHY
(a) Coronation souvenirs, 1952
(b) Glasgow, 1953

(c) Royal tour of Nigeria, 1956

(d) Stirling University, 1972

Cousins of the House of Windsor

APART from giving her name to an age, Queen Victoria was also the undisputed 'Grandmother of Europe'. During their twenty-one years of marriage she and Prince Albert produced nine children, who in their turn brought thirty-nine offspring into the world. The fertility of the House of Saxe-Coburg-Gotha helped to promote that intermingling of royal blood that was so prominent a characteristic of the 'crowned heads of Europe' before the outbreak of the First World War. In 1914 the British royal family was linked by ties of blood and marriage to the Kaiser of Germany, the Tsar of All the Russias, the King of Spain, the King of Romania, the King of Norway, the King of Greece, the King of Denmark, the King of Belgium, the Tsar of Bulgaria, the Crown Prince of Sweden, the Duke of Teck, the Grand Duke of Hesse, the Duke of Saxe-Coburg-Gotha, the Duke of Schleswig-Holstein, the Duke of Brunswick and a further assortment of Princes and noblemen. By 1922 the Yugoslav royal family had also joined the charmed circle.

The international ramifications of the House of Saxe-Coburg-Gotha survived the family's change of name to the more reassuring and Anglophone 'Windsor' in 1917. The events of the First World War, however, which had precipitated this change, also swept the Romanov and Hohenzollern cousins off their thrones. Bolshevik revolution and the apparently uncontrollable spread of socialism to many parts of Europe provided a real and potential challenge to the surviving monarchies, and even George V, who epitomized sound common sense, wondered whether he might be the first and the last monarch of the newly founded House of Windsor. His anxieties were, however, misplaced. His granddaughter, Queen Elizabeth II, has now reigned for a quarter of a century, and there is certainly no reason to anticipate the demise of the British monarchy. The royal cousins of the House of Windsor, however, have not all enjoyed equivalent success, something which would doubtless have surprised the aged Queen Victoria had she been able to foresee it.

The old Queen had kept contact with her extended family through an impressive display of intense interest and emotional involvement which manifested themselves in letter-writing, present-giving and entertaining. It would be naive, however, to suppose that anything like a royal Mafia existed, working effectively behind the scenes, and circumventing the traditional channels of diplomacy. Though Queen Victoria's children and grandchildren kept family ties alive, they were, in the last resort, merely the gilt on the gingerbread of power politics. No amount of cousinly correspondence between King-Emperor, Kaiser and Tsar in 1914 could have averted a war to which the governments of the great powers, with some show of reluctance, found themselves committed. A royal visit could harmonize with a diplomatic manoeuvre here (like Edward VII's famous trip to Paris in 1903), or a private letter could touch upon a delicate problem there, but not much more than that.

Nor were Queen Victoria's family connections inevitably benign. Through her genes the crippling and apparently incurable illness of haemophilia was transmitted, via her female descendants, to the male heirs of the Tsar Nicholas II and King Alfonso XIII of Spain. In the former case the survival of the Tsarevich Alexis, the long-awaited son of the Tsar and the Tsarina Alexandra, was of such vital importance to the Romanov dynasty that the power of the disreputable monk

Rasputin to tide Alexis over his many crises became indispensable to the royal couple. Rasputin resisted attempts to oust him from his privileged position, and eagerly bolstered Nicholas's and Alexandra's belief in the benefits of autocratic rule. This in turn encouraged further criticism of Tsarism, and fed reformist resentment. Though Rasputin was murdered by a nephew of the Tsar in 1916, his intimate association with the Russian royal family certainly helped to discredit it in the eyes of the nation. Queen Victoria was thus partly responsible for the fall of the Romanovs.

The Spanish royal family also suffered from haemophilia, this time transmitted by Princess Ena of Battenberg, a granddaughter of Queen Victoria, who married Alfonso XIII of Spain in 1906. Of their four sons, the first and the fourth were haemophiliac, and the second son was born a deaf-mute. Only the third son, Don Juan (the father of the present King of Spain, Juan Carlos), enjoyed good health. Queen Victoria's genetic legacy thus helped to alter the order of the succession in modern Spain, for the Prince of the Asturias, the eldest son of Alfonso and Ena, bled to death in 1935 following a car crash in Miami and, with the disabilities of the second son Don Jaime rendering him unsuitable, Don Juan's branch of the family was favoured by General Franco in 1966 when Juan Carlos was sworn in as the future monarch and head of state.

Apart from these medically unfortunate genetic links with two of Europe's royal Houses, the British royal family had close contact with other powerful relations. One such relative was the German Kaiser Wilhelm II, the grandson of Queen Victoria through her eldest daughter Princess Victoria. Ascending the throne of Imperial Germany in 1888, Wilhelm had carried out his duties as Queen Victoria's grandson with panache, genuine affection and a little melodrama. He had, however, been deeply mortified by the easy and apparently condescending bearing of his uncle King Edward VII. In these two relationships were reflected the Kaiser's love–hate relationship with Britain, emotions which were perhaps never reconciled even during his exile in the Netherlands after his abdication in 1918. The Kaiser found his diffident and unpretentious cousin King George V far easier to get along with than the late King Edward, and, when in 1911 the former invited him to the unveiling of Queen Victoria's memorial, he replied with considerable warmth:

You cannot imagine how overjoyed I am at the prospect of seeing you again so soon and making a nice stay with you ... You are perfectly right in alluding to my devotion and reverence for my beloved Grandmother ... Never in my life shall I forget the solemn hours in Osborne at her deathbed when she breathed her last in my arms! These sacred hours have riveted my heart firmly to your house and family, of which I am proud to feel myself a member ... You refer to the fact of my being her eldest grandson: a fact I was always immensely proud of and never forgot.

Though the Kaiser was eager to use this occasion to improve Anglo–German relations, the governments of the two nations made it plain that his visit was, in their eyes, simply a family affair with no political or diplomatic implicatons. The outbreak of the Great War destroyed any family accord, and the Kaiser, antagonized by the Royal Navy's blockade of Germany, swore that 'before he would allow his family and grandchildren to starve, he would blow up Windsor Castle and the whole royal family of England'.

The Tsar of Russia, Nicholas II, lacked the flamboyance and the sometimes aggressive verve of his cousin the Kaiser. In personality he had much more in common with George V, and in appearance the two men were so remarkably similar that when they met there were often awkward moments over mistaken identity. King George felt warmly towards the Tsar, telling Queen Victoria in 1894 after Nicholas's wedding to Princess Alix of Hesse (another grandchild of the old Queen, and the future Tsarina Alexandra): 'Nicky has been kindness itself to me, he is the same dear boy he has always been to me and talks to me quite openly on every subject.'

As a result of the Great War Wilhelm II was doomed to twenty-two years of exile, but Nicholas II and his whole family were murdered by the Bolsheviks in July 1918. King George V never forgot or forgave this outrage, and, when Ramsay MacDonald formed the first Labour government in 1924 and wished to recognize Soviet Russia, he told the new Prime Minister 'how abhorrent it would be to His Majesty to receive any representative of Russia, who, directly or indirectly, had been connected with the abominable murder of the Emperor, Empress and their family, the King's own first cousin'.

The Kaiser and the Tsar were the only cousins of the House of Windsor to lose their crowns as a result of the Great War. When the future Queen Elizabeth II was born in April 1926, however, there was a whole crop of royal cousins who were destined, within two decades, to share the fate of the Hohenzollerns and the Romanovs.

Though Greece was declared a republic in 1924, George II regained his throne in 1935 after a plebiscite (which critics said had been manipulated by the army) had recorded a 97-per-cent vote for the restoration of the monarchy. King Alfonso XIII of Spain and Queen Ena were not so fortunate. Their wedding in 1906 had been attended by an ominous portent when an anarchist threw a bomb at the royal couple's coach as they were returning from the Church of San Jeronimo in Madrid to the Palacio Real. The explosion killed twelve spectators and injured over a hundred more, and the shaken Queen stepped out of the carriage with her shoes and the train of her wedding dress stained with blood. The royal show went on, however, and the Prince of Wales (the future George V) proposed his cousins' health at the ensuing luncheon though later admitting that 'it was not easy after the emotions caused by this terrible affair'.

By 1930 Alfonso's reign had become discredited by its close association with the dictatorship of General Primo de Rivera – whom the King once proudly introduced as 'my Mussolini'. In 1931 Alfonso was forced to agree to democratic elections in the municipalities and to the Cortes. Early returns from the municipal elections showed sweeping successes for republican candidates, and soon crowds were in the street demanding Alfonso's abdication. The King was obliged to leave Spain, though prudently refusing to abdicate or to renounce his rights. The Spanish royal family scattered to different parts of Europe and America, and Alfonso and Ena separated. Though the ensuing Republic was destroyed by Franco's Fascist rebellion in the civil war of 1936–9, the Generalissimo chose not to restore the monarchy, but ruled in its place.

The Balkan cousins of the British royal family fell like skittles as a result of the upheavals of the Second World War. King Peter II of Yugoslavia went into exile in 1945, Simeon II of Bulgaria was deposed in 1946, and King Michael of Romania abdicated in 1947. These monarchs' thrones were engulfed by the rising tide of Communism in Eastern Europe, a tide carried to full flood by the victorious advance of the Soviet armies at the end of the war. Michael of Romania prolonged his reign by prudently changing sides on 24 August 1944, for which he received the praise of the Allies and the Soviet 'Order of Victory'. In 1947 he came to London to attend the wedding of his cousin Princess Elizabeth, and at the same time became engaged to Princess Anne of Bourbon-Parma. On his return to Bucharest, however, he was faced with a demand for his abdication from the Democratic National Front government, which disapproved of the prospect of a Romanian royal wedding. On 30 December Michael signed a document of abdication and went into exile.

Michael of Romania was the grandson of Queen Marie, the daughter of Queen Victoria's second son Alfred, Duke of Edinburgh. Marie had been a restless member of the British royal family, and so clever, conceited and melodramatic that she had been nicknamed 'Missy' by her relatives. Queen Marie had made her contribution to Balkan stability in the inter-war years through her family connection: she was herself Queen of Romania; her eldest daughter (also Marie) married King Alexander of Yugoslavia in 1922; her second daughter Elizabeth married George II, King of Greece; and her eldest son became King Carol II of Romania in 1930.

The House of Windsor shared in the family celebrations of these events. In 1922 the future King George VI (then Duke of York) had represented the British monarchy at the wedding of Princess Marie of Romania to King Alexander of Yugoslavia. Queen Marie was grateful for his presence and wrote to his father, King George V: 'Everyone much appreciated that you sent one of your sons and were awfully pleased . . . Somehow your boy in some ways reminded me so much of you, though he has exactly May's [Queen Mary's] smile, but his movements were yours, and his hands.'

A year later the Duke of York attended the christening of the first offspring of this marriage when he was invited to Belgrade to stand as *Koom* (godfather) to the future King Peter of Yugoslavia. The royal christening service had little in common with its more prosaic British equivalents. The Duke of York, who was somewhat shy, was obliged to receive a set of hand-embroidered underwear from the child's parents. He was also responsible for the baby during the rituals, a responsibility that was dramatically put to the test when the aged Patriarch, on receiving Crown Prince Peter for baptism, promptly dropped him in the font, whence he was rescued by his vigilant *Koom*. The Duke of York, having triumphantly survived these tribulations, wrote to tell his father: 'You can imagine what I felt like carrying the baby on a cushion. It screamed most of the time which drowned the singing and the service altogether.'

While the House of Windsor survived the trauma of

Edward VIII's abdication in 1936, its Balkan cousins were visited with a variety of misfortunes even before the cataclysm of the Second World War. Crown Prince Carol of Romania (the future King Carol II) renounced the throne in 1925 for the sake of his divorced mistress Madame Lupescu. Carol's career had been packed with scandal, causing his father, King Ferdinand, to say of him on his deathbed, 'Carol is like a Swiss cheese, excellent for what it is, but so full of holes'. Carol's five-year-old son Michael was proclaimed King in 1927 after Ferdinand's death. Three years later Carol was reinstated as monarch, but was deposed in 1940 by the Romanian dictator Antonescu and went into exile; Michael became King once more and reigned for seven years.

The Yugoslav royal family, linked by marriage to the House of Windsor, had a similarly disturbed history. In 1934 King Alexander I was assassinated by a Croatian nationalist in Marseilles while on a state visit to France. His son, King Peter II, succeeded him and in 1941 had to face the Axis powers' assault on his country. Peter showed enough martial enthusiasm to fight on with his armies, even though his uncle and godfather, King George VI, had once asked him whether a slender gold charm that he wore was part of the uniform of the Royal Yugoslav Air Force, and on receiving a negative reply had said 'Take it off. It looks damned silly and damned sloppy.' When the Yugoslav forces were defeated, Peter went into exile and studied International Law at Cambridge University. The valiant part played by the Yugoslav Communist party in resisting the Axis occupation meant, however, that by the end of 1945 it was Josip Tito, not King Peter, who was the leader of the newly proclaimed Federal People's Republic. The deposed monarch went into exile in the United States where he died some years later.

The Bulgarian royal family were connected with the House of Windsor through their common blood links with the Saxe-Coburgs. The two World Wars, however, saw Bulgaria fighting on the side of Germany. In 1943 Tsar Boris III died mysteriously after a visit to Hitler at his East Prussian headquarters; a regency was proclaimed for Boris's six-year-old son Simeon. Tsar Simeon's reign lasted until 1946 when a referendum showed that 92 per cent of the electors wanted to scrap the monarchy. Simeon and his mother left the country, which was subsequently declared a People's Republic. Ex-Tsar Simeon seems to have thrived in exile; he eventually married the Spanish heiress Margarita Gomez-Acero y Cejuela, and he and his wife apparently fit easily into the charmed circle of the international jet-set.

The Second World War also nearly destroyed the Belgian monarchy, founded by Queen Victoria's beloved uncle Leopold of Saxe-Coburg. In 1940, with the German armies marching into his country, King Leopold III ordered his troops to capitulate and decided to let himself be made a prisoner of the Nazis. Leopold's action and his allegedly pro-German sympathies not only antagonized large numbers of his subjects, but also opened up a deep rift with the House of Windsor. King George VI, who had insisted upon staying on in London during the worst days of the blitz, bitterly resented Leopold's activities. Although Leopold abdicated in 1950, in favour of his elder son Baudouin, the rift with the British royal family did not immediately heal, and in 1952 it was widely noticed that the new King of Belgium declined to attend George VI's funeral, sending his brother Albert instead. King Baudouin and Queen Elizabeth II subsequently reconciled their familes' difference and in 1963 the former paid a state visit to London.

The Greek royal family has also suffered a turbulent history in the twentieth century: in 1913 King George I was assassinated by a madman in Salonika; four years later King Constantine I was deposed after a *coup* by army officers who favoured supporting the Allies in the Great War; his successor, Alexander, died in 1920 as the result of being bitten by a monkey; Constantine I returned for a brief two years' reign, but then abdicated in favour of his son who ascended the throne as George II in 1922 only to be ousted by the declaration of a republic in 1924.

The republic lasted until 1935, when George II was restored. In 1940 Mussolini's forces invaded Greece but were beaten back and humiliated. A year later the German army swept in to crush Greek resistance. Although the Allies liberated Greece in 1944, the country was then plunged into five years of bitter civil war between Communist and monarchist forces. George II died in 1947, before the civil war had ended, and it was left to his younger brother, Paul, to reassert the position of the monarchy. King Paul's reign, which lasted from 1947 to 1964, was marked by accusations against him of right-wing sympathies. His German-born Queen, Frederika, also aroused considerable controversy over her alleged autocratic tastes and the suspicion that she had mishandled a royal fund raised during the civil war for the relief of refugees.

King Paul of the Hellenes died of cancer in 1964, and was succeeded by his twenty-three-year-old son Constantine. The new King was good-looking and engaging, and had appropriately won a gold medal for yachting in the 1960 Olympic Games. In the year of his accession, Constantine II married the beautiful Princess Anne-Marie of Denmark and there were high hopes that the new monarch could preside over an orderly and democratic Greece.

In 1967, however, the 'Colonel's' *coup* brought back right-wing authoritarian government to the country. On 13 December 1967 Constantine, who had previously endorsed the *coup*, attempted to rally loyal support to overthrow the real rulers of Greece. He failed abjectly and within twenty-four hours had fled to Rome with his family. Although the Colonels' regime was overthrown in July 1974, the monarchy was not restored along with democratic government. In a referendum later in 1974, 69 per cent of those who voted in a 76-per-cent turnout were opposed to the restoration of the monarchy, though 31 per cent voted for the King's return.

Ex-King Constantine and his family now live in London, which is appropriate enough in view of their close links with the House of Windsor. The first King of Greece, George I, had been a brother-in-law of King Edward VII. Edward's son, the future King George V, had entertained warm feelings for his Greek relatives and in 1882 had visited them in Athens while training for the Royal Navy on a world cruise aboard H.M.S. *Bacchante*. Prince George, who was a somewhat immature seventeen-year-old in 1882, loved Queen Olga of Greece like a second mother, and recorded in his diary a tearful account of their parting: 'We had to say goodbye to darling Aunt Olga and cousins. We all cryed, very much, we have spent such a delightful time here.'

As a result of these strong emotions a warm royal correspondence continued to flow between Greece and Britain. King George of Greece (Uncle Willy to the family) wrote long and affectionate letters to Prince George, sprinkled with homely descriptions like 'my dear old sausage' and 'my dear old pickled pork'. Apart from these appetizing endearments, a new and more tangible link was forged in November 1934 when Prince George, Duke of Kent, the third son of George V, married Princess Marina of Greece.

An even more significant bond was created in 1947 when Princess Elizabeth (the future Queen Elizabeth II) married Prince Philip of Greece. Although at first sight this match seemed to symbolize an exotic union between two very different countries, the royal couple's ancestry had a great deal in common. Philip was the son of Prince Andrew of Greece and Alice of Battenberg. Through his mother he was descended from Queen Victoria's second daughter, Princess Alice; his father was the son of King George I and Queen Olga of Greece, and a nephew of Edward VII's wife, Queen Alexandra of Denmark. Prince Philip's family name was

Mountbatten, a prudently anglicized version of Battenberg. He had moreover been educated at Gordonstoun School, and had served in the Royal Navy during the Second World War, rising to the post of First Lieutenant aboard the destroyer HMS *Whelp*.

As mankind enters the last quarter of the twentieth century, the cousins of the House of Windsor that have kept their thrones are clustered in northern Europe, in Belgium, Denmark, Sweden and Norway. There is, for the moment, one exception to this geographical grouping – that of Spain. The vacant golden throne of Spain has been occupied since late 1975 by King Juan Carlos, who came into his inheritance when Generalissimo Franco died in November of that year. Juan Carlos and his Queen, Sophia of Greece, have three children. As Spain slowly dismantles the stifling structure of Franco's Fascist state, the new King and his Queen have no guarantee that their reign will be either lengthy or tranquil.

The three Scandinavian monarchs can look to a more secure future, despite the dominance of social democracy in their kingdoms and the occasional ominous rumblings of republicanism. All three trace a direct line of descent from Queen Victoria, though that is no longer any kind of insurance against constitutional upheaval or even dethronement. On the other hand, the royal families of Scandinavia have democratized in earnest, and bicycling in public and undertaking education in state institutions are symbols of their generally informal and unpretentious life-style.

The Swedish royal family are descended from one of Napoleon Bonaparte's marshals, Jean Baptiste Bernadotte. During the twentieth century the Swedish throne has been dominated by two monarchs, Gustav V (1907–50) and Gustav VI Adolf (1950–73). Gustav V's long reign was marked by his open pro-German sympathies and his insistence that Sweden should remain neutral during both World Wars. His son

Gustav VI, who was Crown Prince for forty-three years before ascending the throne, had much more obvious and intimate connections with Britain. His first wife was Princess
Margaret of Connaught, a granddaughter of Queen Victoria,
who bore him five children. Following her death, he married
Lady Louise Alexandra Mountbatten in 1923. Gustav's
second wife was a great-granddaughter of Queen Victoria, the
sister of Princess Alice of Greece and Earl Mountbatten, and
an aunt of Prince Philip, Duke of Edinburgh. Queen Louise
adapted herself well to the relaxed style of the Swedish royal
family, being happy to stroll around Stockholm in ordinary
clothes, and describing herself as a 'housewife' in the National
Health register.

Gustav VI's private pastimes were essentially academic
and intellectual, a far cry from the robust sports and unsavoury dalliances of some of his royal relatives. He was, for
one thing, a distinguished archaeologist, and led a number of
'digs' in Italy, Greece, Egypt and China. He was also a
member of various illustrious scientific societies – including
Britain's Royal Society.

When Gustav died in 1973 the crown passed to his grandson, his eldest son having been killed in a plane crash in 1947
and his second son being as yet unmarried and thus unlikely
to produce an heir. King Carl XVI ascended the throne of the
Swedes, the Goths and the Wends amid much speculation
that he would prove to be the last of Sweden's monarchs. On
the other hand, Carl and his four lively and glamorous sisters
continue to prove that they are very much in tune with the
modern world. Princesses Margaretha, Birgitta, Désirée and
Christina have travelled widely and made marriages outside
of royalty and across international frontiers. Their lack of
prudish convention was perhaps best demonstrated by Princess Christina's departure for Radcliffe College in Massachu-
setts which, according to one Stockholm newspaper, was

likely to be 'a fun-packed year of good fellowship and colle-
giate love affairs'.

Queen Margrethe of Denmark has also been educated
abroad. She spent some time at a girls' public school near
Basingstoke, where, she recalls: 'I was in the top form for
three terms and made some very good friends.' She later
attended Girton College in Cambridge, and studied sociology
at the London School of Economics. She is a keen amateur
archaeologist and used to accompany her grandfather King
Gustav VI of Sweden on Italian 'digs'. Margrethe is married
to a French ex-diplomat, now known as Prince Hendrik; they
have two sons. She is quite evidently a self-assured and intelligent monarch, who, though rejecting stuffy convention,
sees the need for a certain amount of protocol: 'It's a frame-
work to make things easier. For instance, fifty people can't
go through the same doorway all at once. Someone has to go
first.'

Like her cousin, Queen Elizabeth, Margrethe is a great-
great-granddaughter of King Christian IX of Denmark, who
reigned from 1863 to 1906 and was known as 'the Grandfather of Europe'. Christian's daughter, Alexandra, became
the Queen of Edward VII and thus the 'darling Motherdear'
of the future King George V. Alexandra's sister Dagmar married Tsar Alexander III of Russia and was the mother of Tsar
Nicholas II, and her second brother was invited to become
King of Norway in 1905. The international connections of
the Danish royal House of Oldenborg were hence second only
to those of Saxe-Coburg-Gotha.

King Haakon VII of Norway was elected to the throne of
newly independent Norway as the result of a plebiscite in
1905. Though a Danish prince, he became the founder of the
first Norwegian royal House for 600 years. Haakon died in
1957 at the age of eighty-five, by which time he had become
the world's oldest and longest-reigning monarch.

Haakon married Princess Maud, a daughter of King Edward VII and Queen Alexandra, in 1896. Queen Maud died in 1938, two years before Norway was overrun by the Nazis. Haakon and his ministers escaped to Britain, where they set up a government-in-exile and established the Free Norwegian forces. The King's stubborn fight against the German invaders did much to ensure the popularity of the Norwegian monarchy after the republican agitation of the pre-war years. Olav V, who read international law and politics at Balliol College as a young man, succeeded to the throne in 1957. His son, Crown Prince Harald, has married a commoner Sonja Haraldsen; they have one son and one daughter.

The existence of seven monarchies in Europe may, at first sight, seem a ridiculous anachronism in 1977. In a world dominated by the republican form of government, and in an age when men have set foot upon the moon and probed even farther afield in space, Kingship could be seen as an absurdity and an irrelevance. The surviving European monarchies have, however, shown themselves able and willing to adapt to changing circumstances and to more challenging times. Without wishing to promote a theory of monarchical-Darwinism, it might be argued that we are witnessing a survival of the fittest royal families. Whether this resilience is in any measure due to an inherited and shared adroitness is, however, another matter.

J. H. PLUMB

Royal Residences

OVER the last thousand years the functions of monarchy have changed dramatically and the castles, palaces and houses which have belonged to royalty tell that story in brick and stone as vividly as any words can do. Windsor Castle and the Tower; Westminster Hall and the Abbey; Inigo Jones's Banqueting Hall in Whitehall; St James's Palace; Buckingham House, now Palace; the beautiful royal residences within easy reach of London, some totally lost like Nonsuch, others carefully preserved like Kensington Palace, Hampton Court and the delectable Dutch House at Kew; others such as Greenwich, now a hospital, and Eltham, almost a ruin, betwixt and between. Scotland too has its grand royal fortresses: Stirling; Linlithgow; its palace of state, Holyroodhouse; its hunting lodges like Falkland and its home of retreat, Balmoral. All of these have been a part of the ever-changing setting of the British monarchy. In England too the monarchy has often felt a need to escape from its great castles and palaces and live more simply: George IV built Brighton Pavilion; Victoria and Albert escaped to Osborne in the Isle of Wight; Edward VII adored Sandringham and so did his son and grandson. Fortresses, palaces, homes, these the monarchy has needed during the passing centuries, but only Windsor Castle embraced all of these functions. It is the grandest, the most historic and the most symbolic of all the royal residences illustrating as no other castle or palace can the varied ups and downs of the monarchy.

William the Conqueror needed to dominate the lower Thames valley as well as London, the richest, the most vital part of his new kingdom, so he raised the great white Central Keep of the Tower of London where the Romans had long, long before built a fort to block off the river approach. Farther up the valley he built another great stone tower at Windsor. For centuries both remained royal palaces as well as royal fortresses. Each grew vaster with the passing years; each was ringed with inner and outer walls which linked one great tower to another. Some of these were quite sumptuous within – brilliant with tapestries and the finest furniture of the age, and used frequently by the King and his Court – others were military bastions. The Tower and Windsor remained royal Houses for 500 years. Henry VIII added new rooms at the Tower for Anne Boleyn, but in the end this castle was too restricted, too hemmed in by London. It lacked space for expansion and it possessed no park. Windsor had both, yet Windsor too had its ups and downs. The Tudors, apart from Elizabeth, who built a long gallery (now it houses the royal family's books) in which she could stride up and down on a wet day, had little use for it – they preferred St James's and Hampton Court. By Charles II's day it had become very run down. He built a new suite of state rooms which still survives, although altered. It comprises some of the state rooms now open to the public. Yet they too were soon neglected and Queen Anne preferred a small house by the side of the castle when she drove out from London to enjoy the hunting.

It was fortunate that George III's grandfather, George II, had rarely used Windsor since George III refused to live in any palace which his grandfather had used; that is why the magnificent palace of Hampton Court, the small Kensington Palace and St James's are no longer lived in. Instead they have become royal museums and offices, or they provide apartments for members of the royal family or officials of the Court. The main function, however, of Kensington Palace and Hampton Court is a public one, creating a setting for some of the treasures of the royal collections of paintings, porcelain, statuary, tapestries and furniture. Hundreds of thousands of people visit them every year.

George III grew very fond of Windsor and he built the great terrace on which he loved to take the air on the arm of his Queen. He would stop and chat happily to the boys from Eton or people from the town. But it was his son, George IV, who created the castle we know. George IV was an extravagant, compulsive builder and collector whose mountainous debts and self-indulgence have been a fabulous boon to posterity. He encouraged Nash to remodel the West End of London – Carlton Terrace, Regent Street, Regent's Park with its exceptionally fine terraces – a truly grandiose conception in urban planning. It still brings grace and dignity to London in spite of the wanton destruction of Regent Street in this century. All his life George IV built: Carlton House, alas now vanished, he totally remodelled; the oriental fantasy of Brighton, the Pavilion, one of the most original buildings in Europe, was his conception; and when, in his middle age, he succeeded his father, he set to work on Windsor.

He chose as his architect Jeffrey Wyatt, whose vision was as grandiose as his master's. The great medieval Round Tower was raised so that it now dominates the sky line. The old buildings were treated with great sensitivity, but the great Quadrangle was Wyatt's work. It houses an astonishingly long corridor – 550 feet long – that links the state-rooms with the Queen's private apartments, providing a setting for many of George IV's extensive collections as well as those of his forebears and descendants. Perhaps the most nostalgic collection displayed here is the one put together by the Queen's father, George VI, a collection of medals and orders that recall the days of his father and grandfather, when Europe glittered with them.

Among the glories of Windsor are the three great drawing

rooms – the red, the green, the white – all lead one to the other and provide a regal setting for those state occasions which are a part of the duties of monarchy. They contain many masterpieces of the royal collection, many of them purchased by George IV – magnificent French furniture, some of the finest French bronzes, exquisite porcelain and, of course, great paintings. These are rooms of state, used both for entertaining visiting heads of state and for other important royal occasions. In a sense they are semi-private, quasi-official, appertaining rather to the monarchy than the Queen as a private person. Her private rooms are simpler: here dog baskets, children's toys and television sets mingle with fine furniture; along with some outstanding masterpieces there are family photographs and portraits. And also everywhere there are books. The effect is of a comfortable country home belonging to a family which has lived there time out of mind, a warm, domestic corner in a building that is dedicated to the majesty of monarchy. And indeed one of the most colourful traditional ceremonies of the British monarchy takes place at Windsor, when the procession of the Knights of the Garter, England's oldest and most distinguished order of chivalry, winds its way to its Chapel of St George in the Lower Ward, one of the finest Gothic churches in Britain, in which the magnificently carved stalls of the knights, ablaze with heraldry, have seated generations of Britain's most famous men. Their heraldic plates, reaching back into the Middle Ages, decorate their stalls.

One of the great attractions of Windsor is its vast park, in which the royal family can ride. They can relax and escape the hungry attention of the public in the privacy of the gardens at Frogmore; or they can slip over to the Royal Lodge, inhabited by George IV whilst Windsor Castle was being reconstructed, where the Queen Mother now lives. Windsor was, during the Second World War, the royal family home, and the Queen's father found some relief there from the strains of wartime London by indulging his very active passion for gardening. But not for long – the government at Westminster demands, as it always has done, the monarch's presence.

Hence Buckingham Palace. This is the formal setting of monarchy, as Whitehall was in Stuart days, or Westminster in the Middle Ages. These were two great palaces destroyed by fire and never rebuilt. St James's took their place for a time, but George III would not live there and he bought Buckingham House near by from the Duchess of Buckingham, extended it and furnished it with outstanding British furniture and magnificent pictures by Italian artists of his day, particularly Canaletto, as well as with old masters. The Buckingham Palace we know, however, was created early in the reign of Queen Victoria, and naturally, as in everything else, the Prince Consort had a hand in it. The large balcony that overlooks the vast entrance was his idea. There, for several generations now, seething crowds have rejoiced with the royal family, not only over British victories (and nowadays in our sad decline one forgets how many there have been, even in this century), but also over those great events of family life which monarchy must share with the people – marriages and births.

Buckingham Palace is the executive centre of the monarchy. Here the Queen receives ambassadors, statesmen, incoming and outgoing politicians; the Prime Minister every Tuesday when Parliament is in session and she in London; here she entertains, every year, literally tens of thousands of her subjects, from intimate lunch parties for distinguished men and women from all walks of life to the vast garden parties that are a feature of London's summer season. Such activity needs a complex, highly efficient staff. The Queen's staff has a worldwide reputation for the smoothness and ease with which it operates the complicated programmes of the royal family. And, like St James's Palace, much of Bucking-

ham Palace is an office block. It also houses magnificent suites
of rooms – throne rooms, ballrooms, reception rooms etc. –
for formal occasions; only a small fraction of this enormous
palace can the royal family really call its own.

But it is an office block with a difference: every corridor,
every room, possesses some object, some picture which catches
the eye – not always, but usually, with delight. Perhaps the
most remarkable room is the picture gallery, created in the
nineteenth century to house some of the most valuable old
masters in the royal collection. Actually I did not find the
room pleasing – too long, too narrow – but such a reaction
is quickly dispelled by the almost unbelievable quality of the
paintings. Wherever the eye turns there are masterpieces of
the highest quality – Rembrandt, Rubens, Cuyp – too long a
list to catalogue. At one time these were seen only by the
privileged, a fortunate scholar or, when lent out, at an occasional grand exhibition at the National Gallery or Royal
Academy. Now, however, many of these great masterpieces
are frequently available to the public. After the war the
Queen decided that she wanted more people to enjoy her vast
inheritance of art – pictures, drawings, sculpture, furniture,
bronzes, armour, china, glass, stamps – and she created the
Queen's Gallery from the bombed ruins of the Royal Chapel
at Buckingham Palace. In the exhibitions that have been
mounted there, the Queen herself has taken a most active
interest for, like her mother, she is very fond of paintings. In
fact, she has made greater additions to the royal collection
than any of her predecessors since Prince Albert. Her pur-
chases have been mainly paintings associated with the royal
family: a brilliant miniature by Samuel Cooper of Hugh May,
who was responsible for the suite of rooms at Windsor built
by Charles II; a very fine Kneller of George I's intelligent
Turkish servant, Mahomet; two outstanding Blanchets of the
last two Stuarts, Prince Charles Edward and Henry, Cardinal
York, as well as many others. Indeed the Queen has continued

and extended the practice of her mother, who purchased the grave and moving picture of Charles I at his trial by Bowyer, and her grandmother, who rarely missed an opportunity to acquire objects which had belonged to her ancestors. The Queen, again like her parents, who commissioned a splendid series of paintings of Windsor Castle by John Piper, has given her support, as has her husband, not only to modern traditional artists such as Edward Seago, but also to less conventional but perhaps more outstanding painters – L. S. Lowry (and this before the great boom in Lowrys started), Graham Sutherland and Sidney Nolan amongst others. However, unlike her mother, the Queen has been less drawn to the decorative arts although her appreciation is keen enough: the Queen Mother has brought together a quite remarkable collection of early Chelsea porcelain. In this way much that might have been lost to foreign buyers has been saved to bring delight to hundreds of thousands of the public at the Queen's Gallery. This royal heritage has always demanded very great knowledge, care and understanding for its conservation and its proper cataloguing by scholars of the highest repute. The Queen is, in a sense, the director of one of the world's greatest museums, which requires a large staff of curators. It is an aspect of monarchy that we tend to forget, ignoring the constant detailed attention and endless decisions that so vast a collection of masterpieces in all forms of art requires. Rembrandts, Vermeers, Holbeins, drawings of Raphael, of Leonardo, of Michelangelo and countless others fill these palaces in which the public functions of monarchy take, or used to take, place: the royal palaces of state as one might term them. But every monarch from William the Conqueror to Elizabeth II has required a refuge – a place of refreshment and peace where the burdens of state are diminished if not obliterated. And the Queen has two homes that belong essentially to her rather than to the monarchy: one, built by her great-great-grandmother, at Balmoral in Scotland; the other, Sandringham in Norfolk, built by her great-grandfather, Edward VII.

Balmoral is finer, more romantic, enjoying one of the most splendid settings in Britain, tucked in the valley of the Dee in Aberdeenshire, and surrounded by the wild mountain scenery of the Cairngorms. And now, with Sandringham open to the public, Balmoral is the royal family's last citadel of privacy. True, when the royal family is not in residence, the grounds – or policies, as the Scots call them – are open to the public, but the house is not. The castle in its design has echoes of the castles of Thuringia which Prince Albert knew as a boy; nevertheless the building possesses a very strong, individual personality. Its success was immediate, for it was quickly imitated on a small scale by rich Victorian bankers, merchants and industrialists who were establishing homes in the Highlands. Balmoral was far more successful than Prince Albert's design (with Sir Thomas Cubitt's aid) of the marine villa at Osborne.

The castle sits foursquare in its magnificent setting of woods, mountains and swiftly flowing river. No detail was too small for Prince Albert's attention and, in consequence, the craftsmanship is exceptional. The castle is adorned with finely executed bas-reliefs of St Hubert (the patron of hunting), St George (of England) and St Andrew (of Scotland) by John Thomas, which, with the increase of interest in Victorian art, are much more admired now than they were a generation ago. And the same is true of furniture and furnishings. In Queen Victoria's day every table, every chest, was cluttered with photographs, watercolours, drawings, mementoes of people and places that she loved to keep, and these tended to mask the effectiveness and the very high quality of the design of so much of the decorations and furnishings of Balmoral. The famous tartan carpets, so frequently dismissed, are of a most beautiful light green that seems to draw into the castle the green and blue light of the landscape around it. Indeed nowadays a sense of light pervades the royal apartments at Balmoral. The furniture of light woods (pine and maple), designed by Prince Albert, with silver hinges of the entwined initials V and A adds to the effect. Even the candelabras, supported by Highland chieftains in Parian marble, seem totally appropriate: certainly they are not heavy and ponderous, quite the reverse. Of course there are some rather depressing, over-ornate, over-Gothic rooms, too heavily decorated with richly carved wood. The ballroom, main staircase and the entrance hall are rather foreboding, but the general effect of the castle is light, warm and beautiful: the scale remains intimate and domestic. Apart from the main reception rooms there are no large rooms. In Queen Victoria's day a minister was always in attendance, and his suite, used now by the Prime Minister or other members of the government on their visits, is somewhat austere, even modest, as are the majority of the rooms, including those used by members of the royal family. For an historian it is quite moving to look at the narrow bed upon which have slept Prime Ministers from Disraeli and Gladstone to Edward Heath and Sir Harold Wilson: in fact many of England's great and not so great statesmen for over a century.

Most monarchs are driven from time to time by a need for greater privacy, but few felt this so deeply as Queen Victoria. She loved Balmoral and the Highlands. She and her husband often took long rides across the mountains, staying incognito at lonely and modest inns. Some of these jaunts provided the happiest days for Queen Victoria. She loved the rain, the mist, even the cold. She and her husband also created a retreat at the Shiel of Altnaguisach, some miles from Balmoral. Basically it was a large crofter's cottage, but by some mysterious alchemy they managed to give it something of the air of a small Victorian house. When Prince Albert died, in order to share her grief only with her younger daughters and the ever-faithful servant John Brown, Queen Victoria plunged farther into the mountains and built what might have been a villa from Wimbledon, the Glassalt by the side of Loch Muick – a wild, gloomy, romantic place. The villa remains much as she left it: the sitting room looks uncompromisingly at the rocky mountainside beyond the narrow, dark-watered lake; on the bedhead of the four-poster where she lay and grieved, a watch case of Prince Albert's still lies; the china she used – beautiful Minton decorated with leaping salmon – is still on the dressing table. And on the hills near and far are the cairns which she made her family build to celebrate the great events of family life. All of these places, the cottages and the cairns, make delectable picnic areas where the royal family can be entirely by themselves and achieve that dearly sought but rarely found privacy. They, as Queen Victoria did, love the Highland life – the dress, the games, the music and the dances – and each year, as in Queen Victoria's day, the castle echoes with the sound of piping and stamping feet when the gillies' ball is held. Here at Balmoral the tempo of royal life is different, and one can easily imagine with what relief they arrive there in the summertime.

As well as Balmoral, the Queen has one other palace in Scotland, which performs the same function as Buckingham Palace in England – Holyroodhouse at Edinburgh, an ancient palace of the Scottish Kings, which was lovingly restored and completed by her grandfather and grandmother. Each year the Queen spends some time in Edinburgh and now occasionally uses Holyroodhouse to entertain visiting monarchs. To embellish the royal rooms the Queen has brought together a distinguished collection of modern Scottish artists. Both for state occasions and private retreat, Scotland is largely visited in the summertime. The royal family also needed a house nearer to London – but a house, not a palace – and Sandringham in Norfolk has for four generations now fulfilled that need.

Sandringham was the creation of Edward VII during his long years as Prince of Wales. He tore down the old and not very distinguished Georgian house that was there and replaced it with a long rambling house, built in warm brick, full of nostalgia for Tudor architecture yet emphatically belonging to the nineteenth century. It is best seen from across the lake in autumn when its colour harmonizes with the dying leaves of red, gold and brown of the trees and woods that surround it. Often at this time of the year in Norfolk the sky is a pellucid blue, windless, cloudless. At such times Sandringham reaches a kind of perfection.

The interior of the house is a great surprise. There is the typical vast, rather gloomy, *porte-cochère*, under which carriages can draw up, and naturally one expects to enter a great entrance hall with an imposing staircase down which royalty might sweep. Not at all. The door leads straight into a comfortable sitting room, which the King used after dinner for cards and gossip. It is not large, and is rather crowded, and might belong to a dozen of the country houses in Norfolk. Monarchs of nineteenth-century Europe, such as the German Kaiser and the Russian Tsar, must have been astounded by the absence of grandeur. (However, if the house was not on an imperial scale, the shooting was probably the finest in England and as good as any in Western Europe.)

To be frank, neither the furnishings nor the pictures at Sandringham are very distinguished. Edward VII did not have much of an eye for art, but he and his wife knew how to create a sense of solid comfort and the atmosphere of at least two of the rooms is exceptionally warm.

The dining room certainly expresses solidity and comfort: it is dominated by an enormous mahogany dining table, with stout, very stout, fluted legs, surrounded by a suite of large chairs, which look comfortable enough to see one through the long nine-course dinners that Edward VII loved too well; yet, although of the highest craftsmanship, these chairs look ponderous. On the walls are a series of tapestries partly based on works by Goya, given by the King of Spain to Edward VII. Nevertheless there is a heaviness about this room that perhaps is dispelled only when the table gleams with silver and candlelight.

One of the most charming rooms at Sandringham is the Queen's sitting room, whose walls are covered with a delightful embossed paper. It looks towards the west and the windows draw in the golden light of the setting sun. It is, in consequence, a nostalgic room, recalling Edwardian afternoons – serene days before the great catastrophes struck Europe. But by far the most beautiful room in Sandringham is the white, gold and blue drawing room that instantly recalls the elegance and sophistication of Queen Alexandra and the influence which the Russian court had on her taste. Her sister was the Tsarina of Russia and, like her, Queen Alexandra became a passionate collector of the great Russian master craftsman Fabergé. Edward VII, to please her, had all the animals at Sandringham, including their dogs, modelled by his workmen as a surprise present. It was at Sandringham too that the Queen's grandfather lived for so many years as Prince of Wales and as King, in a very small, cramped cottage, York Cottage, where all but one of his children were born, because he refused to dispossess his mother of the main house. And he was also to die at Sandringham, as did his son King George VI. Indeed Sandringham has been the centre of the royal family's private life for most of this century. Many Christmases and many New Years have seen royal gatherings there, the crowds watching the royal family walk to the church, which possesses an astonishing silver altar and pulpit presented to Edward VII by an admiring American, whom he had never met. And Sandringham is also the home from which the first Christmas message was broadcast to the empire by George V and the first television message by Elizabeth II: an event which every year reaches millions of homes. In many ways Sandringham has been the most familial of all the Queen's houses and palaces.

Unlike Windsor Castle or Buckingham Palace – or perhaps we should say to a very much greater extent than – the Queen's homes at Balmoral and Sandringham are centres of considerable economic and commercial activity: forestry, farming, horticulture, every aspect of sophisticated exploitation of their agricultural resources takes place, but always with the keenest consideration for the conservation of the natural beauty of the estates. Without a highly efficient utilization of their resources, these estates would be too great a burden, not only on the public, but also on the private resources of the Queen. They have never been run so efficiently as they are today.

The monarchy may seem to some to be both lavish and expensive, but this is not really true if the monarchy and its functions are seen in their proper perspective. No head of any western European country is permitted to live modestly (nor of Eastern Europe for that matter, and certainly not the President of the United States): status demands a proper setting. Neither the private apartments in the palaces nor the private homes are excessively large or grand. They are royal, certainly, as they should be, so long as the country remains attached to its monarchy, and that is for the foreseeable future. In essence, the Queen is the guardian, not the possessor, of a magnificent royal heritage, built up over the centuries; a royal heritage which is also a national one.

The Queen's Succession

CONSIDER the styles and titles of the Queen. 'Elizabeth II, by the Grace of God, etc . . .' and already, in the second phrase, one is falling into a legal and spiritual fiction. It is not by the Grace of God that the monarch rules. If it were so, the present Stuart heir would have at least as good a claim, and he is the present Duke of Bavaria, a member of the Bavarian provincial assembly and a lover of trees, and also a man who has the good sense not to give interviews even when you write and say, of course truthfully, that you would really like to talk to him about Bavarian affairs and Bavarian forests.

The Queen rules by virtue of 12 & 13 William 3, cap 2, 1702, which established the Hanoverian succession, this being necessary since poor Queen Anne, though having given birth to thirteen heirs, had seen them all die. So if there is any godly grace appertaining to the monarchy, it is only such part of that grace as is agreeable to Parliament. The British constitution works because it is founded on compromises, even with God. With the divine right of Kings, you at least knew where you were. The Act of 1702, being human, was fallible and, worse, it was uncertain. It was uncertain as recently as 1936 when, Edward VIII having abdicated, George VI became King and his children heirs to the throne. It might have been supposed that Princess Elizabeth, in the absence of a brother, became heir presumptive, but the question was raised whether, in strict law, Elizabeth and her younger sister Margaret Rose might not be co-heirs. It was put forward

– in *The Times*, no less – that if the new King were to die the result might be 'Co-Queens', on the analogy of *The Gondoliers*.

Now, the idea of a disputed succession seems so extravagant, and is so thoroughly forgotten, that one is inclined to dismiss it as nothing more than a little diversion added to the sad play that the monarchy had been acting out that year. Kings had not been so interesting since Shakespeare. There was confusion. The evening Edward VIII abdicated audiences did not know what to do when the National Anthem was played, as it then invariably was, in cinemas. Some audiences spontaneously stood to attention. Some sang. Others did not have the heart to stand, or sing, or even stay still, but shuffled out. Perhaps some were unsure which King God should be asked to save. Mr George Black, manager of the General Theatre Corporation and Moss Empires, instructed the managers of all houses to play 'Land of Hope and Glory' instead of the National Anthem. There was also superstition. It was recalled that a strange fatality had pursued the eldest sons of the first monarchs of new dynasties throughout English history. The eldest son of James I of the House of Stuart died before his father. The eldest son of Queen Anne, by her consort of the House of Denmark, died before he came to the throne. The Duke of Clarence, eldest son of Edward VII, first monarch of the House of Saxony, predeceased his father. And now Edward VIII, eldest son of the first monarch of the House of Windsor, had abdicated before his coronation. And after this confusion and this superstition came a tiny uncertainty over the succession, mentioned by *The Times*, which, so far as I have been able to discover, first raised and then principally sustained the topic. A small paragraph, in the middle of a page, remarked that things were not quite as they had been in the seventeenth and nineteenth centuries, when Anne and Victoria, only daughters, had become heirs presumptive. No rule of succession as between *two* daughters of a monarch

12. Badminton, 1972

13. THE BALCONY AT BUCKINGHAM PALACE
(a) (*top left*) King George V's Silver Jubilee, 1935

(b) (*bottom left*) The royal wedding, 1947

(c) (*above*) The wedding of Princess Anne and Captain Mark Phillips, 1973

14. (a) Princess Elizabeth, 1929

(b) Queen Elizabeth, 1973

15. The royal family at the
Queen's Silver Wedding, 1972

16. GROWING UP
(a) The Duchess of York with her daughter Elizabeth, 1926

(b) With King George VI, Queen Elizabeth and Princess Margaret at Sandringham, 1943

(c) Broadcasting to the nation's children, 1940

(d) Training with the ATS, 1945

(e) With her mother and sister at the Braemar Gathering, 1946

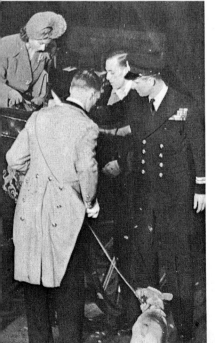

(f) With Lieutenant Philip
Mountbatten, 1946

(g) Leaving for the
honeymoon, 1947

17. FAMILY LIFE (*right*)
(a) After the christening
of Princess Anne, 1950

(b) Family lunch at
Windsor Castle, 1969

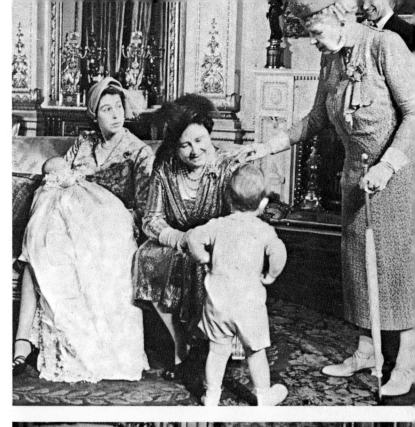

(c) Leaving for
Balmoral with
Prince Charles
and Princess
Anne, 1950

(d) With Princess
Anne, 1951

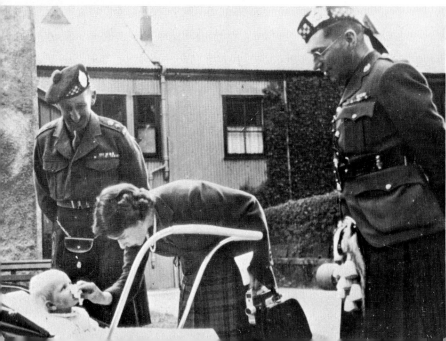

(e) At Balmoral, 1953

(f) With Prince Edward and Prince Andrew, 1971

(g) Square-dancing during the tour of Canada, 1951

(h) Dancing at the annual Ghillies' Ball, Balmoral, 1972

(i) At Badminton, 1973
(j) Prince Philip describes a marathon driving event,
Royal Windsor Horse Show, 1976

18. THE QUEEN'S HORSES
(a) Leading in Carrozza ridden by Lester Piggott after winning the Oaks at Epsom, 1957
(b) Windsor Horse Show, 1975

(c) In the paddock at Windsor with William, 1959

(d) Riding with Princess Margaret and friends in Badminton Park, 1959

had yet been laid down in England, and it was hoped that statutory provision would be made to remove any possible doubt in the matter.

It may have been an obscure, arcane doubt, but unfortunately it did have constitutional and legal substance. More unfortunately still, the principal proponent of the view that there was no rule of succession between two female heirs was John Horace Round, who had been adviser to the royal family on genealogy. By 1936 Round was dead, but he did not lack supporters. S. H. F. Johnston, of the University College of Wales at Aberystwyth, declared that the Act of Settlement (that of 1702 previously alluded to) would undoubtedly need to be amended before anyone could be considered heir presumptive. A correspondent to *The Times*, signing himself only 'Yorkist', argued that there was no precedent for conferring the inheritance on an older as opposed to a younger sister. (The rule of primogeniture among male heirs was of course established and in no doubt.) So, he went on, upon the next demise of the Crown, the choices would be four:

1. An abeyance of the Crown, on the analogy of the peerage law.

2. A partition of the empire between the two sisters, on the analogy of the real-estate law.

3. Two dynasties, whose heads would agree to occupy the throne in alternate reigns.

4. Co-Queens. ('Yorkist' was the author of the *Gondoliers* proposition.)

He also quoted, most eloquently, from the great judgement of Chief Justice Crew in the case which removed the office of Lord Great Chamberlain, after 500 years, from the male line of the De Vere family which had held it since 1133. 'Time', said Crew, CJ, 'hath his revolution; there must be a period and an end to all temporal things, *finis rerum*, an end of names and dignities, and whatsoever terrene; and why not of De Vere? For where is Bohun? Where is Mowbray? Where is Mortimer? Nay, which is more and most of all, where is Plantagenet? They are entombed in the urns and sepulchres of mortality.' The House of Windsor, plainly, could go the same way, or so he was implying.

This called forth a brisk letter from 'Lancastrian', who, relying rather on sense than on law, said the Crown of England *could* not go into abeyance. The analogy of an abeyant peerage would not do, since in that case the Crown was there to decide whether it should grant the peerage to one of the co-heirs or refuse to act at all. But, if the Crown itself became abeyant, there would be no Sovereign to terminate the abeyance. It was impossible, Lancastrian appeared to be arguing, and therefore it could not be allowed to happen.

There the matter could have ended. The authority of letters written from Aberystwyth or under pseudonyms is not constitutionally great. But on 19 December 1936, nine days after the abdication, *The Times* devoted two whole columns to an article which ran right down one side of the leader page and turned to the next. There was, it said, practical urgency in the matter, which had troubled students of the constitution for more than forty years. The article said the succession to the Crown was established by the Act of Settlement, and before we go on with the arguments expressed in *The Times* it might be as well for us to see exactly what that Act has to say. These are the pertinent words:

... for default of issue of the said Princess Anne and of his Majesty [Prince William of Orange] respecting the crown and regall government of the said kingdoms of England France and Ireland and the dominions thereunto belonging the royall state and dignity of the said realms and all honours stiles and titles regalities prerogatives powers jurisdictions and authorities to the same belonging and appertaining shall be remain and continue to the said most excellent Princess Sophia [Electress of Hanover] and the heirs of her body being Protestant.

That, said *The Times*, created what was known as a limitation to heirs-general, which was to say that, if the eldest male line ended in an only daughter, as with Victoria, the inheritance was hers. But the ambiguity arose when the line ended in a family of sisters, for in that case the ordinary law of England (though not of Scotland) gave them equality of rights. If the inheritance was a peerage – of which the remainder would indeed go to heirs-general – then that peerage went into abeyance. If it was real property, it was divided. The late J. H. Round had examined this ambiguity in 1892 on the death of the Duke of Clarence, the son of the then Prince of Wales. Round saw that at that moment only the deaths of the Prince of Wales himself and of his younger son the Duke of York stood between the three daughters of the Princes of Wales and the throne. (As it happened, the Prince of Wales survived to become Edward VII, and his son the Duke of York to become George V.) But, Round had concluded, if those two lives had fallen, there would have been no precedent in English law for preferring one of the three daughters, even the eldest, to her sisters. Round said that only an amendment to the Act of Settlement could resolve the issue, and the failure to pass such an amendment 'might involve a vacancy of the Throne'. He also said: 'It is no doubt generally believed that, in the event of the succession opening to two or more sisters, the Crown, in England, would always pass to the eldest sister as of right. But it is not a question of general belief; it is a question of an Act of Parliament.'*

The Times then set out the arguments against the Round thesis, but first made a concession and asked a question. The concession was that, if the Crown were a peerage or real property, then Round's case would be unanswerable; but it was neither, and there were arguments based on the Crown's own nature and history which might justify a different treatment.

* J. H. Round, *Studies in Peerage and Family History*, London, Archibald Constable & Co. Ltd, 1901.

But then came the question. To whom, to what body, should such arguments be addressed? Suppose a demise of the Crown did occur and two sisters were the heirs. The question between them could not be addressed to Parliament, for Parliament formally consists of Crown, Lords, and Commons – the King in Parliament – and therefore, without a monarch, Parliament could not exist. Nor could the question be decided by the judiciary, because no judge was a judge until he had taken the oath of allegiance – and that would be an oath to whom? So the sole body with power to act would be that assembly of peers, privy councillors, members of Parliament, the Lord Mayor and aldermen of London and those other gentlemen of quality whose normally formal task it was to draw up the proclamation of a new King. In such a case they could hardly do other than resolve themselves into a judicial tribunal to interpret the Act of Settlement. They would no doubt listen to legal argument, but there was no reason why they should prefer principles derived from any one branch of the law to the exclusion of others. The position would be complicated by the Statute of Westminster, 1931, the preamble to which did lay down that changes in the succession should require the unanimous consent of all the self-governing Dominions.

The legal complexities were becoming hilarious, so the learned authority of *The Times* turned to Sir William Blackstone for sanity. He, writing in 1765, had said boldly:

Among the females, the Crown descends by right of primogeniture to the eldest daughter only and her issue; and not, as in common inheritances, to all the daughters at once; the evident necessity of a sole succession to the Throne having occasioned the royal law of descents to depart from the common law in this respect.

Unhappily, Blackstone's principal authority for this statement was Blackstone.

There were, however, certain historic precedents that lent

colour to the doctrine of female primogeniture. Colour was the word, and this was plainly the opinion of the learned writer. The first was the Scottish Succession case of 1292. Edward I of England, called in to judge between the claimants to the Scottish throne on the death of the Maid of Norway, first held that the Crown was indivisible, and then awarded it to the representative of the eldest female line. Before forming this decision he took counsel with the magnates of both kingdoms; and it might therefore be supposed with some reason that his judgement was based not on the municipal law of Scotland but on the general body of international feudal custom, and so might be applied to the interpretation of an English Act. *The Times* arguments then progressed from feudalism to Henry VIII, among whose several Succession Acts was one which did define the meaning of heirship to the Crown. This was 25 Hen. 8 cap 12, which bastardized the Lady Mary and proceeded to settle the Crown on the Lady Elizabeth and the heirs of her body, 'and so on from issue female to issue female, and the heirs of their bodies, by course of inheritance according to their ages, as the Crown of England hath been accustomed and ought to go, in case where there be heirs female of the same'.

The trouble was that there was no such custom. Like Blackstone's assertion later, this was based on precedents that had no existence. Parliament is Sovereign in its particular Acts, but even Parliament cannot, by a simple statement, create and bring into existence something which never did exist.

'Having failed', said *The Times*, three quarters of the way through its excursion into constitutional obscurities, 'to find a tolerable analogy for the Crown either in a dignity, or in an office, or in a real estate, it is worth while to consider whether the true analogy is not with the combination of all three.' To find such a combination it was necessary to trace the three elements back through history until they fused in a single institution, and this was the feudal 'tenure of barony' as it existed before 1290. A tenant by barony, and especially an Earl, always held by this tenure and united in himself three essential characters. He was the governor of his fief, with duties to the King; he had corresponding rights over his land and its tenants; and he had the title of Earl or Baron. In all this he was analogous to a Sovereign. He was a petty King. Therefore it was worth considering what had happened when an Earl died, before 1290, leaving several daughters and no son. The succession was determined by a compromise between two conflicting forces. The King was concerned to ensure that the governing functions of the barony should continue, and therefore tried to keep it united in one hand. The heiresses were interested only in the property, and, their rights being equal, they tended to share it out. The accepted compromise, for which the leading authority was the Earldom of Chester case of 1232, was that the sisters should divide the property but that the husband of the eldest should remain the responsible overlord for the whole fief, with the others rendering through him the services to the Crown due for their shares. That is to say, all that could be divided (the property) was divided, but the indivisible, the seat of government, went to the senior co-heir. It might therefore be argued that, on a demise of the Crown leaving co-heiresses, the eldest was entitled to so much as was indivisible – which was necessarily, in the case of the Crown, the whole.

The Times then concluded:

On these highly artificial lines it is possible to construct a case for regarding the Princess Elizabeth as sole heir-presumptive to the Throne. But, considering that each Dominion now has equal rights of interpreting the Act of Settlement, it is by no means of so conclusive a character as to ensure that the six interpretations shall be identical. If embarrassing differences of legal opinion are not to arise in the Empire at a time when there is no authority in existence with power to resolve them, it seems essential to pass a new Succession Act without delay, declaring whither, in default of male heirs to his Majesty, the Crown is to pass.

There it was, a case of the utmost complexity, subject to the minutest argument and equivocation and learning, a constitutional lawyer's delight. *The Times* completed its duty in this grave matter by publishing one retort from Wales, from R. Stewart-Brown of Bryn-y-Grog. The Chester case of 1232, he said, was admitted by everyone to have shown that the husband of the eldest female co-heir was entitled to be, and was, Earl of Chester. But it did not decide that if the eldest co-heir had not been married she would have been Countess of Chester. The case therefore seemed to be a precedent only for the proposition that, if Princess Elizabeth were married when the question of succession to the Crown arose, her husband would be entitled to be King, with one half of the empire. It was getting near Christmas 1936. The government took legal advice. Nothing more was heard for a while.

What might have happened? It must be allowed, first, that the constitutional issue was a substantial one. It must be admitted, secondly, that it was pure Camelot. If the Princesses Elizabeth and Margaret Rose had become co-Queens, the character of the monarchy might not be what it is. If the empire had come to be divided, by the time that moment came, in 1952, what was divided would have been held only on very short leases. The position of the Earl of Snowdon, particularly now after his separation from Princess Margaret, would be incapable of solution even by the minutest raking over medieval precedents.

What happened was in the highest traditions of English constitutional practice. Nothing happened. It was by far for the best. On 29 January 1937, after Commons questions on arson in Wales, horse-breeding, and intrusion by the Press into privacy, Sir John Simon, Home Secretary, rose to answer a planted question:

MR MANDER (Wolverhampton East, Liberal): Whether it was proposed to introduce legislation to amend the Act of Settlement with a view to making clear that the Princess Elizabeth was the sole heir to the Throne and did not share it jointly with her sister on the analogy of the Peerage Law.

SIR J. SIMON: No, Sir; there is no reason to do so. His Majesty's Government are advised that there is no doubt that in present circumstances her Royal Highness the Princess Elizabeth would succeed as sole heir.

That was that. Very wise. But there *was* doubt. Elizabeth II, having in 1952 been proclaimed and in 1953 crowned, and having since reigned, is undoubted Queen, but she is so a little by the grace of Sir John Simon, as well as by that of God.

Royal Occasions

ALMOST everyone who visits Britain, and particularly London, comes with the intention of seeing something of the pageantry which attends the British monarchy. On a fine day, between 5,000 and 10,000 people will gather to watch the changing of the guard at Buckingham Palace, and 2,000 or 3,000 spectators will surge around the entrance to Horse Guards Parade in busy Whitehall to see the changing of the Queen's Life Guard by members of the Household Cavalry Regiment. Annual occasions, such as the State Opening of Parliament in the autumn, and the Trooping the Colour ceremony, which takes place on the Queen's official birthday – not to mention a Coronation, a royal wedding, or a jubilee – are events people will travel across the world to see.

The hope of catching a glimpse of the Queen herself is a major incentive, but the brilliance of the ceremonial surrounding her is without parallel anywhere, and has evidently lost none of its power to draw the crowds.

It may be that such rare sights and sounds are even more attractive in an age of levelling politics, especially when they can be enjoyed with a clear conscience. People can happily watch a royal show, knowing that it no longer represents the power of an oppressive monarchy but is rather a vivid and colourful expression of common traditions, a living review of British history.

This is the clue to the importance of royal ceremonial in our time. Because the Crown is above and outside politics, it still retains an almost magic power (possessed by few Presidents) to unite millions of people in a common emotion; and the huge television-viewing figures for a major royal occasion sufficiently demonstrate that the majority of people are happy to forget their differences for a while and enjoy the heritage shared by all.

The ceremonial functions of the British monarchy have grown up gradually in the course of hundreds of years, and the Queen inherited most of them from her ancestors. If what happens at royal events appears to have the unalterable pattern of Mosaic law, this is, however, largely due to the skill and sense of fitness of the organizers and performers. In fact, although precedents provide useful guidelines, changes are often made according to the nature of the ceremony and its location, and sometimes quite new procedures are invented. One important innovation, which obviously needed much careful consideration, if only from the point of view of security, was the introduction of royal 'walkabouts' – the first of them in this country took place during the Silver Wedding celebrations in the City of London.

It is part of the Queen's achievement that, in the matter of ceremonial as in so many other areas of her life, she has, with her advisers, steadily moved with the times – anticipating the need for a change in style but allowing it to take place naturally, at a pace which poses no threat to continuity and stability. But, while the forms of some royal ceremonies have undergone gradual adjustment during the Queen's reign, the nature and size of the audience for many of them has changed radically, owing to the rapid growth of television over the past twenty-five years. In former years the royal family could expect exhaustive coverage of their public activities in the Press, with the artists of such magazines as *The Illustrated London News* adding an imaginative touch to the work of photographers and film cameramen; and the Queen's father and grandfather had become accustomed to the presence of radio commentators on ceremonial occasions. But in the 1970s it is an accepted fact that most major royal events will be seen on television, 'live' or later, not only in the United Kingdom but throughout the Commonwealth and all around the world. In the full glare of television lights, the Queen will have to play out her ceremonial role in June 1977, not before a few thousands assembled in St Paul's Cathedral, but before a world audience, which for such an occasion as the Silver Jubilee will certainly be numbered in hundreds of millions. This fact must surely add greatly to the strain for all concerned. Moreover the need to accommodate cameras and provide them with an unimpeded view of the entire event is an additional problem for those who have to arrange such ceremonies.

Thanks largely to television, all of us now feel we have seen the Queen at close quarters, and each of us probably has a personal anthology of favourite moments. For me the golden splendour of the Abbey at the Coronation with the Queen, a slender, youthful figure, about to assume the weight of the Crown remains a vivid memory; so does her radiant smile in the Coronation coach afterwards, and, on a different level, the appearance some years later of a relaxed family group on the steps of St George's Chapel at Windsor after Christmas Morning Service – a kind of animated Christmas family portrait, arranged very much with the television audience in mind. Some people will particularly value brief glimpses of other members of the royal family on such occasions – the Queen Mother, perhaps, or the royal children when they were younger. To an extent never before possible we have all been able to share highlights in the royal family's life – to admire, and sympathize too perhaps – as they play their inexorably public roles in the various episodes of the royal drama.

Apart from the principals, who are the performers in that drama, and who are the producers? These are the questions we now consider, as well as offering some idea of how television plays its part, in this modern age, in the time-honoured rituals of royalty.

Those who organize royal ceremonial cordially dislike theatrical analogies. They point out that, however spectacular a royal event may be, it only takes place in order that the Queen may carry out some essential part of her royal function; the fact that such things are tourist attractions and make good television should, in their view, be regarded as incidental. Moreover, they argue, all those who take part in these events do so for good historical reasons and are not present merely for the sake of their picturesque costumes.

All arrangements relating to the public appearances of the royal family come within the province of the Lord Chamberlain (Lord Maclean) as head of the household. The Private Secretary and his department deal with the Queen's routine engagements, her constitutional activities and state visits overseas, but the *Comptroller of the Lord Chamberlain's office* deals with the great majority of ceremonial occasions; even on those major state occasions organized by the Earl Marshal, the Comptroller is responsible for ensuring the safe arrival and departure of the royal family together with such items of regalia as may be required.

The Comptroller (Lt-Col. Sir Eric Penn, KCVO, OBE, MC) is a busy man. Courteous, clear-headed and extremely articulate, this former Grenadier Guards officer, with the help of a compact team of assistants and secretaries based at St James's Palace, is responsible for the running of the royal palaces in London, in Scotland and at Windsor and for overseeing the royal collections – of pictures, other works of art, and books – as well as for organizing ceremonial events, including those concerning the ecclesiastical role of the Queen as head of the Church of England.

Indeed the first of the events arranged each year by the

Comptroller is the Epiphany Service which takes place on 6 January at the Chapel Royal and at one time marked the end of the Court's Christmas festivities; at this the Queen offers gifts of gold, frankincense and myrrh to commemorate the Adoration of the Magi, the Baptism of Christ and the Miracle at Cana. (The distribution of the royal Maundy – specially minted silver coins – on the Thursday of Holy Week is looked after, as perhaps might be expected, by the Keeper of the Privy Purse.)

Every year the Comptroller will oversee a total of fourteen Investitures – six in Spring after the New Year Honours, and eight in summer and autumn, following the Birthday Honours. The Central Chancery of the Orders of Knighthood, which deals with the detailed arrangements for all such awards, is part of the Lord Chamberlain's office. The Comptroller, or his assistant, personally supervises the sequence of events on these occasions from the arrival of hundreds of rather overawed recipients to their despatch, complete with award, to the waiting photographers in the palace courtyard. It is one of the Lord Chamberlain's men who briefs the recipients on the procedure to follow when they come before the Queen in the ballroom (if the ceremony is held at Buckingham Palace), they who ensure the statue-like presence of dismounted members of the Household Cavalry on the stairways, and the attendance of the Queen's bodyguard of the Yeomen of the Guard in the ballroom together with the regimental orchestra which plays light music as the Investiture proceeds. The efficiency of the arrangements, which combine speed with dignity, commands almost as much admiration as the Queen herself, standing on a dais for about an hour and a quarter and exchanging friendly and well-informed words with all who come before her.

Even larger numbers of people must be dealt with at the annual garden parties – normally three at Buckingham Palace and one at Holyrood House in Edinburgh. These are attended by some 35,000 people. Invitations are handled by a special garden party section of the Lord Chamberlain's office, staffed by girls employed for eight months of each year and known consequently as 'the permanent temporaries'.

Every year brings an average of three 'incoming' state visits to Britain, and these are also a matter for the Comptroller. Preparations normally take from four to six months, owing to the need to consult many people abroad on innumerable details of timing and protocol. The process begins with a call at the Lord Chamberlain's office by the ambassador of the country in question, when the well-established routine of state visits in Britain will be outlined and any desirable amendments will be discussed. In this, as in all other matters pertaining to royal ceremonial, precedent is the guide but is not allowed to stand in the way of change if change seems desirable: one major instance of a departure from established tradition has been the revival during the Queen's reign of state visits at Windsor Castle instead of at Buckingham Palace, but every visit differs from others in detail according to the objectives to be achieved, and the nature and numbers of the visiting party.

Such considerations are of vital importance in arranging the ceremonial transport of the visitors, who will probably take part with the Queen and other members of the royal family in at least one carriage procession. Responsibility for the transport by road of the royal family and their guests belongs to the *Crown Equerry* (Lt-Col. Sir John Miller, KCVO, DSO, MC), who rules over the Royal Mews under the aegis of the Master of the Horse (the Duke of Beaufort) – an honorary office whose present incumbent is, however, a great expert on horses and horsemanship, and so plays an important advisory role. The Crown Equerry looks after the royal family's motor cars, ranging from the four official Rolls Royces to privately owned vehicles, but his main concern is with horse-drawn transport.

Far from being superseded, carriages are now used on a larger number of royal occasions than formerly – on visits to places remote from the royal palaces of London, Windsor and Holyrood as well as on the racecourse at Ascot. The Crown Equerry's own enthusiasm for this stylish mode of transport matches that of the Duke of Edinburgh, and latterly of the Prince of Wales – and it both encourages and reflects a widespread movement in the country as a whole. There are driving classes now at most competitive events where horses are shown, and the British Driving Society, of which Prince Philip is patron, has over 2,000 members, all the more attracted to an elegant hobby, perhaps, as the cost of petrol becomes more and more prohibitive. All this has meant a growth rather than a diminution in the number of people skilled in the many crafts associated with carriages and horses – a state of affairs for which the Crown Equerry is grateful.

Members of the public are welcome to visit the Royal Mews in Buckingham Palace Road on Wednesday and Thursday afternoons, and they do so in their thousands. There they are able to see many of the seventy carriages of many different types which are in the care of the Crown Equerry. From state coaches and state landaus, to the less opulent barouches, phaetons and sociables, they are all in working order – and every possible precaution is taken to ensure that they perform as required on public occasions. In the middle of a dark November night in 1976 the gold state coach itself – which has not been used by the Queen since her Coronation – was drawn by a team of horses to St Paul's Cathedral, in case the Queen should decide to use it for the Jubilee Service in June 1977. Only thus could the Crown Equerry be sure that the coach would be able to negotiate the route, including the inclines of Fleet Street and Ludgate Hill, in safety. It appears that no one working for Fleet Street's newspapers noticed this strange nocturnal apparition or, if anyone did, he was unwilling to admit it.

Those watching the Jubilee procession, like those who visit the Royal Mews, will probably be even more interested in horses than hardware. When it is used, the gold state coach is drawn by eight of the ten grey horses (known as Windsor greys because in Queen Victoria's time horses of this colour were kept at Windsor) now stabled at the Royal Mews. In addition there are twenty bay harness horses. Staffing is on the basis of one man to two horses: the coachmen, postillions and walking grooms, who look so impressive on parade in their scarlet-and-gold or black liveries, also have to cope with all the routine day-to-day chores of the stable.

Though the Crown Equerry will contribute the means of transport to the 1977 Jubilee celebrations, the Comptroller of the Lord Chamberlain's office will be in overall charge of the ceremonial arrangements, as is the case with royal weddings and royal funerals – except for the state funeral of a monarch. This is one of the relatively few very grand occasions which are arranged by the *Earl Marshal*.

The title of Earl Marshal of England has been hereditary in the family of Howard since 1672 and is held by successive Dukes of Norfolk. The office had its origins in Norman times, when the King's Marshal – a marshal occupied a place in a great man's business *outside* the household, parallel to that of the chamberlain *within* it – became one of the chief officers of state. One of his functions was to act as judge in the Courts of Chivalry, and the present-day Earl Marshal presides over the College of Heralds, which regulates all matters concerning armorial bearings and the tracing of genealogies (duties carried out in Scotland by the Court of the Lord Lyon).

Chief of Staff to the Earl Marshal is Garter King-of-Arms. He and the other Kings of Arms – Clarenceux and Norroy-and-Ulster – are the sole authorities for Grants of Arms. They are assisted by the Heralds and the Pursuivants, who rejoice in such splendid names as Rouge-Croix, Bluemantle and Port-cullis and were originally apprentice Heralds. Anyone aspiring to be a Herald must have a good initial knowledge of heraldry and, if accepted as a possible candidate, must wait for up to five years before becoming a Pursuivant. It may seem difficult to understand why there should be many people nowadays interested in a job which still carries a salary established in Tudor times of £17.80 per year (as one Herald put it, 'we have suffered the longest pay-pause in history') but it is a position of much honour and Heralds are allowed to work on their own account in the business of heraldry and genealogy, subjects which, fortunately, are of abiding interest to large numbers of people. Many different kinds of organization as well as many individuals need advice on armorial bearings: one Herald holds an appointment as heraldic adviser to the Football League; another was involved in a Devisal of Arms for the State of Virginia, presented by the Queen during her Bicentennial visit to America; a third is busy developing suitable insignia to display the varying ranks of Maori chiefs. Heralds are also in considerable demand as speakers, with the rapid growth in the number of heraldic societies up and down the country, and they are often consulted by the producers of royal souvenirs.

Originally Heralds acted as messengers between sovereigns, and often superintended jousts, tournaments and other public ceremonies. Part of this latter function survives, for it is they who, under the Earl Marshal, actually make the arrangements for the occasions for which he is responsible. The Heralds can be seen as a body at the State Opening of Parliament when, dressed in their richly embroidered tabards, they occupy a position ahead of the monarch in a procession led by the Earl Marshal and the Lord Great Chamberlain (the officer in charge of the Palace of Westminster), both of whom walk backwards (except, nowadays, down the final flight of stairs after the ceremony is over – a change approved quite recently by the Queen to the lasting relief, no doubt, of Earls Marshal and Lords Great Chamberlain).

The State Opening is the only annual event supervised by the Earl Marshal, though Garter King-of-Arms is responsible, as might be expected, for the Annual Service of the Order of the Garter at St George's Chapel, Windsor. The Earl Marshal comes into his own at the Proclamation, Coronation and state funeral of a monarch. He is also called upon to arrange state funerals accorded to distinguished citizens: the only two such funerals to take place in recent history have been those of the Duke of Wellington and Sir Winston Churchill. In addition the Earl Marshal has organized two Investitures of a Prince of Wales in modern times: those in 1911 and 1969, both held at Caernarvon. It is said that the late Duke of Norfolk, who died in 1975 to be succeeded by his cousin, first indicated the general outlines of the 1969 Investiture to those most closely involved by moving round half a dozen flower pots on the terrace at Arundel Castle. Whether this particular story is true or not, the late Duke was certainly as much noted for his dry sense of humour as for his complete mastery of the job.

Two other groups of people must be numbered among the main organizers of royal occasions: the *police* – who have to concern themselves with many difficult problems, among them security and the marshalling of crowds and traffic – and the *armed forces*, who often have a major part to play at such events. The army is of course more frequently involved than the other services, particularly in London, where it is on show daily, mounting the Guard at Buckingham Palace and in Whitehall, and is seen on many other ceremonial occasions, chief among which, from the army's point of view, is surely the ceremony of Trooping the Colour which takes place every year on Horse Guards Parade on the Queen's official birthday. This superbly disciplined spectacle, attended by the Queen on horseback, goes back to the earliest days of land warfare, when colours were used as a rallying point. Each soldier had to learn to recognize the colours of his regiment in the chaos of battle, and partly for this reason – though also because the colours became a symbol of regimental honour – they would be carried down the ranks at the end of a day's march and escorted to their resting place for the night. The custom of Trooping the Colour to mark the Sovereign's birthday began in 1805 and has continued almost without interruption since then.

Since so many of those who regularly take part in royal occasions are on show for the Trooping the Colour ceremony, this may be a convenient moment to turn from those who organize royal ceremonial to those who perform in it.

Prominent among those who appear in public with the Queen are the *Household Troops*: these consist of the seven regiments of the Household Division with the addition of the King's Troop, Royal Horse Artillery. The role of the *King's Troop* is entirely ceremonial. Stationed at St John's Wood in north London, it was so named by King George VI in 1947 at an inspection of the then Riding Troop, Royal Horse Artillery. The troop owes its existence to the express wish of the King that after the Second World War (by which time all horse artillery batteries had been mechanized) a Troop of Royal Horse Artillery, mounted and dressed in the traditional manner, should once again be seen taking part in the great ceremonies of state. This the King's Troop now does, while it also provides one of London's most brilliant spectacles, when it fires a royal salute in Hyde Park after exercising its privilege, shared only with the reigning monarch, of passing under Marble Arch. On such occasions spectators will see seventy-one horses with six guns gallop into action – a vivid reminder of days gone by, when everything depended in battle on the courage of men and horses. Courage and skill are still needed in plenty by the King's Troop, whose Musical Drive staged at the Royal Tournament and elsewhere is a hair-raising exhibition of brilliant riding and split-second timing.

Considerable riding skill is also needed by the mounted Sovereign's Escort which accompanies the Queen when travelling by carriage: the gleaming helmets and cuirasses (breastplates) of the men, seen from afar, are always the cue for rising excitement along the route. The Escort consists of soldiers of the *Household Cavalry*, which is the collective title of the two senior regiments in the British army, The Life Guards and The Blues and Royals. The Life Guards were formed in Holland by King Charles II just before his restoration to the throne, while The Blues and Royals were created by the amalgamation in 1969 of the Royal Horse Guards – who date back to Cromwellian times – and the Royal Dragoons, who were originally formed in the reign of Charles II. Unlike the King's Troop, these regiments have operational roles as part of the fighting strength of the army – The Life Guards as an armoured car regiment, The Blues and Royals as an armoured regiment – but each supplies a detachment of squadron strength which together make up the Household Cavalry Mounted Regiment based in London and consisting of some 350 men.

Those chosen for this work are given five months in a riding school after their basic military training and generally serve for some three years with the Household Cavalry. Their horses – all black except for the mounts of Trumpeters – are reared in Ireland and have four months' training before they are seen on parade. Much depends on their fitness, so they are very well-fed and well-cared-for, even to the extent of having a month's holiday in the country each year at Pirbright.

As every commentator knows only too well, a treacherous complex of distinguishing traditions and customs has grown up in the Household Cavalry as in other regiments of the Guards Division – the fact that The Life Guards wear scarlet tunics and white helmet plumes while The Blues and

Royals wear dark blue tunics and scarlet helmet plumes is among the more obvious of them. A Sovereign's Escort is made up of four divisions of twenty-four horses, and, when officers, Advance Points, Standard party, Farriers and Coverers are included, consists of 116 horses in all. To preserve perfect dressing in a procession moving at about eight miles an hour (the speed is taken from that of the royal carriage) calls for constant practice on the part of all concerned; the subaltern of the leading division has a particularly difficult job, for he has to look behind him every few seconds for the sword signals given by the Serrefile Captain (at the rear of the second division) to tell him whether he is going too fast or too slow. In command of the escort are the Field Officer of the Escort, who rides on the right of the royal carriage, and the Escort Commander who rides on the left.

Apart from their processional duties, the Household Cavalry mount the Queen's Life Guard in the Front Yard of Horse Guards Parade in Whitehall (regarded as the official entrance to the royal palaces), provide the dismounted detachment which lines the processional route for the annual Garter ceremony at Windsor Castle, stand guard at the entrance of the House of Lords at the State Opening of Parliament and, on ceremonial occasions, within Buckingham Palace itself. Such is the stillness of these figures that many a visitor to the Palace has had to suppress an urge to touch them to find out if they are real.

With such privileges, and the special skills their function requires, it is not surprising that Household Cavalry officers can acquire a touch of grandeur. When the present writer was involved in a television outside broadcast of a major event for which some twenty-five cameras were to be used, he expressed the hope to a Blues and Royals officer that the weather would stay fine for the occasion. 'Ah yes,' was the lofty reply. 'Rain is not very good for our uniforms and of course it could simply ruin your snaps!'

The remaining five regiments of guards are no less proud of their collective and individual traditions. A superficial glance suggests that all guardsmen look the same, with their large black bearskin caps and scarlet tunics. But look more closely. The *Grenadier Guards*, who share the regimental motto 'Honi soit qui mal y pense' with The Life Guards and Blues and Royals, trace their origins back to the mid-seventeenth century and the exiled Charles II. They wear, among other distinguishing marks, white plumes on the left side of their bearskins and single buttons evenly spaced on their tunics, recalling their historic title as 'The First Regiment of Foot Guards'. The *Coldstream Guards* have red plumes on the right side of their bearskins and wear tunic buttons in groups of two, but their motto 'Nulli secundus' may perhaps be taken as a reminder that they began life as Colonel Monck's Regiment of Foot in 1650 – even earlier than the Grenadier Guards. If it were not for breaks in service in the seventeenth century, the *Scots Guards* might claim precedence over both the Grenadiers and the Coldstream Guards, for they were first raised as a personal bodyguard to King Charles I in 1642. However, they were called, before Queen Victoria's time, 'The Third Regiment of Foot Guards', and wear their buttons in threes: they wear no distinguishing plume on their bearskins, because they always stood in the centre of the line.

The other two guards regiments are of more recent origin. The *Irish Guards* were formed in 1900 by command of Queen Victoria, who greatly admired the courage of her Irish troops; apart from the six inches of St Patrick's blue cut feathers or bristle worn on the right hand side of their bearskins, and their groups of four buttons, they are the only regiment in the Household Division to have a mascot on parade – an Irish wolf-hound. The *Welsh Guards* wear on the left side of their bearskins a nine-inch plume of green and white cut feathers. With their buttons grouped in fives, they are the junior regiment in the Household Division, formed in 1915; but like their brothers in other guards regiments they have a proud array of battle honours and personal awards for bravery. All the regiments continue to play an active role in the forefront of the operational army, though they all have tours of ceremonial duty at home.

The Guard Mounting at Buckingham Palace takes place every morning in summer and every other morning in winter. The ceremony involves the old and new guards at both St James's Palace and Buckingham Palace together with a regimental band and corps of drums; and on a fine day it is a brilliant sight for the crowds who gather to peer through the Palace railings. The regiment finding the Queen's Guard for Buckingham Palace also provides the Guard for the Tower of London, where there is a Guard Mounting at noon each day and 'The Ceremony of the Keys' takes place at ten o'clock every evening. There is also a daily Guard Mounting ceremony at Windsor Castle, where the Guard is provided by the Battalion of Foot Guards stationed at Windsor.

Although the major responsibility for the Queen's security in these times is borne by the police, there are other men who have a ceremonial role as bodyguards. The 'nearest guard' is provided by the bodyguard of the Honourable Corps of *Gentlemen at Arms*, founded originally by Henry VIII out of jealousy of the French King's bodyguard. Nowadays the Gentlemen at Arms, with their resplendent scarlet uniforms and white-plumed hats, consist of some thirty-five retired officers of the army or the Royal Marines, and they are regularly seen in attendance on the Queen at palace functions and ceremonies. So too are the Queen's *Bodyguard of the Yeomen of the Guard*, said to be derived from the oldest military organization in the world, founded in 1485. In former times their number included 'Bed-Goers', who had to drive a sword through the royal mattress to make sure it contained no intruder, and 'Bed-Hangers', who had to air and make the royal bed. They were also required to bring the monarch's food up from the kitchens and taste it before their master or mistress did. These services are happily no longer required, but the eighty Yeomen of the Guard, with their characteristic uniform, who are selected from men who have given long and distinguished service in the Forces of the Crown, have an honoured place, with their officers, in the royal entourage, adding greatly to the colour and dignity of royal occasions. A cross-belt distinguishes them visually from the Yeomen Warders of the Tower of London, who were appointed members of the Yeomen of the Guard (Extraordinary) in 1552. The *Royal Company of Archers* have formed the Sovereign's bodyguard in Scotland since the time of King Charles II.

No account of royal ceremonial would be complete without mentioning the music which plays so great a part in it. Each of the regiments of the Household Division has its own highly trained musicians; in addition to the regimental bands, each battalion of Foot Guards has its own corps of drums, about twenty strong and comprising a group of fifers and percussion players, while the Scots and Irish Guards also have some twenty-five pipers. The mounted bands of The Life Guards and The Blues and Royals have always had a strong appeal for the public, and there is always much admiration for the drum horse, invariably a sturdily built creature of steady nerves, who generally carries his heavy load of drummer and two kettledrums through many years of good service. Resplendent in their golden state coats and jockey caps, whenever the Queen or another member of the royal family is present, the trumpeters of the Household Cavalry add the glitter of their fanfares to many occasions. Nor must we omit to mention the numerous other bands of the army, Royal Air Force and Royal Marines which are involved in Royal ceremonial from time to time.

As with musicians, so with people in general. There are very few walks of life which are not represented on occasion in Britain's pageantry. All branches of the three services are frequently called upon, while members of the peerage, the Orders of Knighthood and the Diplomatic Corps, the Sheriffs and Lords Lieutenant, members of national and local government, the Church, the law, academic life and voluntary organizations add their own characteristic ceremonial ingredients when appropriate. All indeed should be able to feel they have some share in the symbolism of our twentieth-century monarchy; and the fact that its symbols are splendid surely befits a Queen who is head of a worldwide Commonwealth which in the late 1970s still numbers some 850 million citizens.

This vast number of people – and all the people of other nations across the world who are interested in the Queen's ceremonial appearances – can now enjoy almost as close participation as those who live in the British Isles – thanks to television. It is during the twenty-five years of the Queen's reign that television has come to occupy its present dominating place as a means of communication, and its cameras have been focused increasingly on the activities of the royal family. In Richard Cawston's 1969 television film *Royal Family*, for example, a great deal more was seen and heard of the Queen's private as well as public life than had formerly been thought desirable; to meet the changing requirements of the age, the manner of the Queen's Christmas Day message has become far more informal than it used to be; television outside broadcast cameras have been allowed to work for the first time in many hitherto closed areas, such as the interiors of Buckingham Palace and Windsor Castle. One hopes that these things have come about because the Queen has felt increasingly able to trust those in charge of royal broadcasts; whatever new ideas they may wish to try out, they learn not to overstep the intangible but nonetheless real boundaries of taste and dignity which still exist, however much the style may change.

Many state occasions had of course been described on radio

before the Queen's accession, her own wedding as Princess Elizabeth to Prince Philip in 1947 among them; there were three television cameras (all at Hyde Park Corner) to witness the Coronation procession of her father in 1937, and newsreel cameras were present in large numbers on that occasion as they had been for many years previously. But the Queen's Coronation in June 1953 was the first great state occasion in British history which could be seen step by step as it happened in millions of homes, and from that time onward the Queen has become more and more accustomed to the presence of television cameras whenever she makes a public appearance.

There was something of a battle before television achieved its Coronation coverage. The presence of TV cameras along the route was never in question, but the royal family, advised by the Duke of Norfolk and the Archbishop of Canterbury, were uncertain about allowing television into the Abbey for the Coronation Service. Would the presence of cameras and cables threaten the dignity of the occasion? Would an element of vulgarity perhaps tarnish the sacred splendour of the ancient ceremony? Nine months before the Coronation, the Palace issued a statement to the effect that the BBC would not be permitted to televise in the Abbey. Only after protracted lobbying, and a demonstration in the Abbey showing how unobtrusive the cameras could be, was there a change of view; once the decision to admit the cameras had been made, the BBC received unstinted cooperation from all concerned – a state of affairs which has persisted between the Palace and the broadcasting authorities to this day.

The televising of the Coronation was an unqualified triumph and showed that the royal family had little to fear if such occasions were handled with due respect and skill: their confidence depended on unobtrusive and un-intrusive camera work, and on a commentary which would be accurate, sympathetic and dignified. What might have happened if a

Richard Dimbleby had not been available to fulfil that role in the testing years between the Queen's accession and his untimely death in 1965 is difficult to imagine. With his meticulous emphasis on 'homework' and ability to marshal his material, his gift for the telling phrase and dramatic sense of timing, he set a truly daunting standard for his successors in the task of commentating on state occasions.

Dimbleby's apparently inexhaustible ability to improvise when things went wrong (which was really fluency in dealing with his mass of 'associative material') was put to its most gruelling test during the television broadcast of Princess Margaret's wedding in 1960. After the ceremony in the Abbey he had travelled with producer Antony Craxton (who has handled most major royal events for the BBC during the Queen's reign) to the Pool of London, where the cameras were to cover the departure of the newly married pair in the royal yacht. As Jonathan Dimbleby has related in his biography of his father, Dimbleby was fully prepared for a twenty-minute delay; in fact fifty minutes elapsed from the opening of the Pool of London section of the programme to the arrival of the Princess. Watching the pictures of river and shoreline offered by Craxton, Dimbleby talked 'smoothly, calmly, eloquently' throughout. 'Few people realized,' said Craxton, 'that what was being seen and said had not been planned in great detail beforehand. Unrelated subjects and objects were somehow, by Richard's description, made into a pattern that at once sounded natural and flowing.'

Although the Palace now fully accept the presence of television, some restrictions are still imposed. At Princess Margaret's wedding, there were to be no cameras forward of the couple at the marriage ceremony itself, to respect the privacy of their feelings at this emotional moment, and a similar decision was made for the wedding of Princess Anne a few years later in 1973. Other limitations have sometimes to be imposed on television outside broadcast producers owing to the need to accommodate the cameras of both BBC and commercial television, not to mention film cameramen and Press reporters and photographers, all of whom try for the best points of vantage. The Queen's Press Secretary (Ronald Allison) needs, among many other qualities, considerable tact as an arbitrator, and is not always able to accept without qualification television's claim to be treated as a special case.

However, there have been instances in recent years when the needs of television have had a direct bearing on the way royal events have been planned – the eavesdropper has now become a participant, to some extent, in the process by which these occasions are prepared. An example of a change of plan suggested by television occurred at Princess Anne's wedding. The Princess herself wanted to dispense with the awning outside the Abbey so that everyone would have a view of her. However, if this had been done, Press and TV cameras would inevitably have been exposed to view. So the TV producer suggested a special design of awning which met the Princess's wishes as far as was possible, and which included cunningly devised 'hides' to accommodate the cameras. The presence of the awning caused only minor adjustments to the planning of the wedding – adjustments of the type now willingly considered by the Lord Chamberlain's office.

In at least one major event during the Queen's reign, the needs of television had a good deal of influence on those designing it. This was the Investiture of the Prince of Wales at Caernarvon in July 1969. Since the present writer was involved as a TV commentator on this occasion, it may perhaps serve as an example of the way such events are prepared.

After the Queen had decided that the Investiture should take place in July 1969, it was the Duke of Norfolk as Earl Marshal who announced the plans for the day at a Press conference in Whitehall. The ceremony would take place, like the Investiture of Prince Charles's uncle, the Duke of Windsor, in 1911, in the castle at Caernarvon, which, a magnificent ruin, is open to the sky. 'What happens if it rains?' asked an apprehensive reporter. 'If it rains,' replied the Duke, with simple candour, 'you will get wet.' In the event there was a slight drizzle but this fortunately did not mar the spectacle.

A major royal event so far from London required planning of a particularly elaborate kind. Almost everyone and everything – the Household Cavalry, the carriages, large units of the army, huge quantities of radio and television equipment, those participating in the ceremony and those invited to watch it in the castle, had to be transported to and then accommodated in a beautiful but remote north-west corner of Wales.

The form of the ceremony itself and of the processions leading to it evolved gradually. The only precedent in this case was the 1911 ceremony, of which careful descriptions and some photographs existed. On the whole the Earl Marshal took the view that such tradition as existed should be preserved; but these ideas were modified by the Constable of Caernarvon Castle, the Earl of Snowdon, who, as an expert photographer and a man of artistic originality, could see that the heavily draped dais used in 1911 would effectively conceal much of the ceremony from those in the castle grounds, let alone the millions who would be watching on television. The theatrical designer Carl Toms designed a dais with a transparent plastic top which would allow spectators and cameras a clear view, and this was eventually adopted.

Over eighteen months before the event took place key members of the BBC TV team went to Caernarvon on the first of many visits. Though dedicated to cooperation with television, Lord Snowdon stipulated that no structure should be built by the reporting media in the castle which might spoil the lines of the walls, and that no piece of equipment should be visible on the skyline. These requirements were met by ingenious use of the many cracks and crevices in the ancient structure. Soon afterwards began the detailed working-out of what exactly would happen, who would move where and when, in the castle on the day.

The timing and pacing of the ceremony was in the hands of Richmond and Somerset heralds from the College of Arms. They made a memorable sight one very wet day in February, six months before the ceremony, walking slowly and solemnly up through the castle, stop-watches in hand. Someone who unwisely approached them was waved aside with an imperious 'Sh! TIMING!'. This was indeed of vital importance, for large numbers of people had to be brought into place before the chief participants made their appearance at the appointed hour. Just one matter which depended on the heralds' timing was the music to be provided by the Master of the Queen's Music, Sir Arthur Bliss. One of the most critical points for him was the presentation of the Prince to the people of Wales at three points in the castle. For this he had to compose a triple fanfare, with linking passages designed to match the time it took to proceed from one presentation point to another.

In the months before the ceremony, various parts of it were tried out separately. For one such rehearsal all the musicians mustered at the Royal Military School of Music at Kneller Hall, Twickenham. There, under the overall direction of the late Lt-Col. 'Jigs' Jaeger, they were spaced out in the grounds at approximately the distances which would apply on the battlements of Caernarvon Castle: one group assembled on the tennis court, another on the roof of a disused air-raid shelter. Sir Arthur Bliss was present to assess the effect of his antiphonal fanfares in the open air.

The royal family were also involved in early rehearsals. One bitterly cold winter's day, representatives of the BBC and ITV television teams were invited to witness a preliminary run-through at Buckingham Palace of the movements involved in the ceremony. Though the weather was uninviting and the ground covered in frost, this rehearsal was held out of doors in the grounds of the palace, where the outlines of the castle had been marked on the grass with white tape. Most of the royal family were there and as they went through the proposed actions, under the instruction of the Earl Marshal, members of the Queen's household and of the College of Heralds stood round noting the movements as they were tried out, and checking the all-important timings.

In the weeks immediately preceding the ceremony, the pace of the preparations increased rapidly. Construction of the dais, of stands to accommodate the large choir and thousands of invited guests, of TV and Press platforms, went on within the castle walls, while, in a specially constructed stockade outside, the broadcasting authorities began to assemble all the equipment they would need on the day. The long series of rehearsals culminated in a complete runthrough on the day before the ceremony, which was of the utmost value to those reporting the event as well as those taking part.

So it happened that on 1 July 1969, the whole world was able to watch a brilliant spectacle carried out with faultless precision. The same process of infinitely careful planning and preparation is applied to every royal event; for the Jubilee celebrations of 1977 it will doubtless result once again in the kind of perfection which has come to be associated with British royal occasions. It will not, however, be a cold perfection.

The Queen's Horses

ON 16 June 1974 cries of 'Vive la Reine' rang out across Chantilly racecourse. The Queen of England had come to watch her three-year-old, Highclere, run in the Prix de Diane. And, as Joe Mercer rode back in triumph after beating all the best French fillies, no Grand National or Derby winner ever received a more rapturous welcome. Royal horses from England had run and won in France before, but Queen Elizabeth II had never been there to watch them, and the loyal citizens of the Republic did not intend to let the occasion pass unnoticed.

As the object of their admiration walked calmly down to greet Highclere in the winner's enclosure, it seemed to her trainer, Dick Hern, far from certain whether the lines of gendarmes would succeed in holding back the half-hysterical crowd. 'It looked like a rugger scrum to me,' Dick said, 'but she just walked through smiling as if it was another garden party.' As Dick, Joe Mercer and their wives flew back that evening, hot and dishevelled but happy and full of well-deserved champagne, the pilot of their chartered aircraft received an urgent radio call. He was to fly straight on to Heathrow, where a car would be waiting to take his four passengers to Windsor Castle. For them it was a perfect, unexpected end to an unforgettable day and, as they and the royal family drank Highclere's health that night, one can imagine the Queen looking back down the years of her association with the sport for which Highclere had struck such a famous blow.

The filly's own pedigree – which her owner-breeder needed no stud book to recall – itself contains many signposts along that road. Forty years earlier Princess Elizabeth's interest in horses was chiefly concentrated on the ponies which she and her sister loved to ride and care for. She was probably not told – or, if she was, took little notice – when her grandfather's racing manager bought a yearling called Feola out of Lord St David's stud. Now an acknowledged expert on thoroughbred breeding and pedigrees, the Queen knows how vital and far-reaching an influence one good prepotent brood mare can have on a stud or indeed on racing as a whole. But, although she may well have known that Feola (carrying Lord Derby's colours because King George V had died in January 1936) finished second in the One Thousand Guineas and third in the Oaks of that year, neither she nor anyone else can possibly have foreseen how much more the mare would go on to accomplish.

For Feola is almost a story in herself. She produced six individual winners, one of whom, Hypericum, won the One Thousand Guineas in 1946. She was the grandam not only of Aureole, perhaps the best racehorse to carry the Queen's own colours, but also of Doutelle who, but for his untimely death, might have been as successful a sire as his cousin. Another grandson, Round Table, whose mother, alas, was sold to America, became one of the best horses ever to race in that country, winning no less than forty-three races and 6 million dollars. So, since Feola was also the great-granddam of Highclere, she certainly deserved to be remembered with gratitude that night at Windsor.

The Queen's abiding interest as a horse-breeder has understandably always been in the royal stud and the mares and horses she inherited from her father. But, in his reign and for part of her own, it was the custom for monarchs to lease for their racing careers horses bred at the National Stud, and it was two of these who gave Princess Elizabeth her first taste of real success on the turf.

In the early years of the war, for security reasons, neither she nor Princess Margaret was allowed to go racing or even to be seen much in public. The rumour that they had been evacuated to Canada was intentionally never denied, so the young Princess was only able to enjoy at second hand the triumphs of Big Game and Sun Chariot, who in 1942 won four of the five Classic Races for King George VI. These two had been bred at the National Stud and were therefore trained not by Captain, later Sir Cecil, Boyd Rochfort (who took over as royal trainer on the death of Willie Jarvis in 1943) but by Fred Darling at Beckhampton. It was there that King George VI, knowing by now his daughter's growing enthusiasm for racing, took her one morning to watch Sun Chariot and Big Game do their final gallops before the Derby and Oaks.

Then sixteen years old, Princess Elizabeth had already begun to take a real interest in the care and stable management of horses and indeed, with only a skeleton staff at Windsor in wartime, she and her sister had to some extent looked after their own. Even in wartime, however, Fred Darling, a strict old-fashioned disciplinarian, never relaxed his rigid standards, and the spotless yard and gleaming horses at Beckhampton were an impressive and memorable sight. So, in a rather different way, was Sun Chariot herself. Always temperamental and unpredictable, she chose that morning to show the black side of her character. Darting off the gallop into a ploughed field, she went down on her knees 'roaring like a bull' and forced her rider Gordon Richards to bale out into the mud. The embarrassed champion jockey told Fred Darling afterwards that it was the first time he had ever found it necessary to polish his boots between first and second lots !

Sun Chariot duly repaid him by adding the Oaks and St Leger to the One Thousand Guineas she had already won.

Strangely enough one of her sons, Landau, was the last horse Gordon Richards ever rode in a race. Half an hour after finishing third on Landau in the 1954 Eclipse Stakes at Sandown he suffered the fall which ended his unique career.

As a student of breeding and equine heredity the Queen no doubt now recalls Sun Chariot's antics without surprise. Captain Boyd Rochfort always said that Hyperion's best offspring were those with a bit of temperament and, in Hypericum and Aureole, the royal stud soon produced two vivid confirmations of that theory. The Queen was often to be reminded of that first visit to Beckhampton. Fred Darling bred and Gordon Richards rode the horse who beat Aureole in the Derby. Gordon often rode in her colours, and it was at Beckhampton that she first met and got to know Lord Porchester who has for several years now been her racing manager.

Hypericum, Feola's daughter by Hyperion and Highclere's granddam, was a positive menace on the gallops at Newmarket and far from easy to steer at any time. She had great ability, however, and in 1946 Princess Elizabeth went down to Newmarket to see her run in the One Thousand Guineas. There were no starting stalls in those days and, as the field lined up, Hypericum suddenly charged the tapes, ejected her unfortunate jockey, Doug Smith, and galloped off in the general direction of her box at Captain Boyd Rochfort's stable, Freemason Lodge. The other runners were kept waiting for nearly a quarter of an hour, which no doubt did them more harm than it did Hypericum, who, eventually having been caught by the driver of the Newmarket fire engine, was reunited with Doug Smith and, setting off in the right direction this time, outstayed the favourite, Neolight, to win in style.

This was the first royal victory in an important race that Princess Elizabeth had ever seen. After the long anxious wait it must have been a thrilling moment, and the big crowd (in those immediate post-war years all English racecourses were packed) gave her a tremendous welcome as she came to greet Hypericum and Doug Smith. The only woman in the winner's enclosure, her small elegant figure was made to look tiny by those of Boyd Rochfort and the King's racing manager, Charles Moore, both of whom were well over six feet tall.

By this time the Princess had been making regular visits to the royal stud, then at Hampton Court, so she came to know not only her father's mares but also their foals and yearlings well before they came into full training. Her own first favourite was Rising Light, who finished fifth in the 1945 Derby (still run at Newmarket and the first she ever watched). She also saw yet another of Feola's daughters, a filly called Angelola, who, though just beaten in the Oaks, had proved herself the best of her sex by the end of the year. And later, when mated with Hyperion, Angelola produced the elegant if rather flashy chestnut colt who was to give the new Queen such a wonderful start as an owner in the first two years of her reign. But the mixture of excitement, disappointment and anxiety which he was to give the young Queen comes later in the story. Her interest in horses and racing had started long before the bright chestnut was foaled, and he was not even the first horse to carry her personal colours.

Although flat racing has always held first place for the Queen, one must not forget her patronage of steeplechasing, which has its roots in one evening at Windsor Castle. It was during a Royal Ascot Meeting, and as usual a large house party had collected. No doubt it mostly consisted of friends of the royal family likely to enjoy the racing at Ascot, but one of the guests would certainly have felt more at home at Cheltenham, Aintree or even Newton Abbot.

Lord Mildmay was then not only the leading amateur rider under National Hunt Rules but almost certainly the best-known and best-loved figure in British National Hunt racing. He never pretended to care much for the flat and, on the night to which I refer, sitting next to Queen Elizabeth (now the Queen Mother), he suggested, with the charm and enthusiasm for which he was famous, that she might enjoy the excitement and novelty of owning a steeplechaser. Lord Mildmay's keenness caught the Queen's imagination and she remarked to her daughter across the table that they might be partners in the venture.

For the world of jumping it was an historic moment, because it would be impossible to exaggerate the value to the winter game of the devoted support which the Queen Mother has given it ever since. And, although her daughter's chief interest was and always has been in flat racing, for her too the decision to buy a jumper proved to be a landmark.

In fact by then the Princess already owned a racehorse. When she married Prince Philip in 1947 the Aga Khan's wedding present had been a thoroughbred filly foal. But, although Astrakhan, as she was called, did eventually win a minor flat race, the Princess's colours had by then already been carried to victory at Fontwell Park by Monaveen, the horse whom she and her mother bought in partnership on Lord Mildmay's advice. Trained by Peter Cazalet, Monaveen won four steeplechases that season and then ran an honourable if somewhat exhausted fifth behind Freebooter in the 1950 Grand National. Princess Elizabeth watched that race, and six years later, as Queen, she went back to Liverpool on the dreadful, unforgettable day when her mother's Devon Loch slipped and fell half way up the run-in with the great race at his mercy.

Poor Monaveen was killed in a fall at the Hurst Park water jump, and earlier that same year the whole world of jumping had been saddened by the death of Lord Mildmay himself, drowned while swimming near his home at Mothecombe in Devon.

It was appropriate that the Queen Mother's great successes

as an owner (her horses have since won over 300 races) should be launched by the brilliant stallion Manicou, on whom Lord Mildmay himself had won six times. Bought for her at the dispersal sale of his horses, Manicou carried the now famous blue and buff colours to victory at Kempton Park and then won the King George VI Chase on the same course before retiring for a successful career at stud.

After Monaveen's death it had been decided that Princess Elizabeth should concentrate on flat racing, leaving the National Hunt scene to her mother. It seemed a sensible and logical division of interests and one which has suited both sides.

In 1952, when King George VI died, the new Queen was already devoted to the running of his stud and the performance of its products on the racecourse. On the death of her grandfather, King George V, Lord Derby had voiced the feelings of the racing world when he wrote, 'it would be a fatal blow ... if His Majesty did not continue to race'. There were no such fears in 1952, and to everyone's delight Gay Time, who had just been bought for the National Stud and leased to the Queen, won at the first Royal Ascot of her reign.

The bright chestnut colt already referred to, by Hyperion out of Angelola, was showing such promise as a two-year-old that he might even provide the new Queen with a Classic victory in her Coronation year. The colt's name had been chosen by the Queen herself. Angelola was by Donatello and, having in mind the golden haloes which the great sculptor used to put around the heads of his saints, the Queen called Angelola's son Aureole. Historically there have been very few good horses with unattractive names but, although this one was both beautiful and inspired, it quickly became apparent that Aureole's many qualities did not include saintliness. He won the Acomb Stakes as a two-year-old but soon became every bit as difficult and temperamental on the gallops as Hyperion's daughters, Sun Chariot and Hypericum.

Bruce Hobbs, who before the war, at the age of seventeen, had won the Grand National on Battleship, became Captain Boyd Rochfort's assistant that year and, together with Harry Carr and a skilful horseman called Frank Holmes, he set about channelling Aureole's explosive and exhibitionist tendencies in the right direction.

Their efforts began to be rewarded next season when, after running well in the Two Thousand Guineas, Aureole ran clean away with the Lingfield Derby Trial. The Epsom Derby that year came just four days after the Coronation, and the story goes that, when one of her Ladies in Waiting asked the Queen if all was well on the morning of the ceremony, she replied, 'Oh yes, the Captain has just rung to say that Aureole went really well'.

The stage seemed set for an historic and supremely well-timed royal triumph at Epsom, but, although Aureole was not quite good enough to provide it, the 1953 Derby nevertheless produced one of the most universally popular results in the long history of the race. For, as Harry Carr drove Aureole into second place a furlong out, the only jockey left in front of him was Sir Gordon Richards, knighted by the Queen in her Coronation Honours and seeking his first Derby winner after twenty-seven unsuccessful attempts. The gigantic Pinza duly helped him fulfil his last great ambition as a jockey and, as soon as Sir Gordon had weighed in, the Queen called him and Pinza's owner, Sir Victor Sassoon, up to the Royal Box to congratulate them. Fred Darling, on whose gallops she had watched Sun Chariot misbehave eleven years before, had himself bred the winner but was alas too ill to be at Epsom. Three days after hearing Pinza's triumph described on the wireless he died, happy at least in the knowledge that he had become one of the very few men ever to have owned, bred *and* trained winners of the Derby.

Beaten again by Pinza in the King George VI and Queen Elizabeth Stakes, Aureole failed to stay the St Leger distance, and all that summer, as his behaviour continued to deteriorate, it was evident that he would be a far more effective racehorse if only he could be reformed.

The Queen has always been ready to try out and encourage new methods of treatment for her animals, and she knew that Doctor Charles Brook, a London neurologist, had successfully calmed several over-excitable horses used at her Coronation. His method consisted, quite literally, in the laying-on of hands and, after discussion with Moore and Boyd Rochfort, the Queen suggested that he should be called in to treat Aureole.

It would be an exaggeration to say that all the horse's mental problems were solved overnight, but, although Aureole never became anything like an easy or phlegmatic character, he took to Doctor Brook at once and used to stand calmly eating hay while the doctor's soothing hands rested on his back and withers. Without any doubt the treatment played an important part in Aureole's brilliant four-year-old career.

Before this treatment, however, since Harry Carr could not make the weight, Aureole was ridden one day at Ascot by Eph Smith, elder brother of Doug. A difficult situation then arose, because, although Carr had always ridden Aureole and had indeed given up much of his winter holiday to ride him out at home, Captain Moore was convinced that the horse went more kindly for Smith.

Captain Boyd Rochfort understandably defended his stable jockey, but in the end the Queen reluctantly followed her manager's advice. Though of course a bitter blow to Harry Carr, and the sort of agonizing decision which owners so often have to make, it turned out to be the right one. Thanks largely to Aureole's exploits – with Pinza now retired he won the Coronation Cup, the Hardwicke Stakes and, most memorable of all, the King George VI and Queen Elizabeth Stakes at Ascot – the Queen became for the first time leading owner in Great Britain. In all these big races Aureole was ridden by Eph Smith who, towards the end of his career, became almost completely deaf. Before the Hardwicke Stakes Aureole bumped his eye in his box and could not see out of that side. 'I am afraid we are in a bad way, Ma'am,' Smith cheerfully told the Queen, 'he's half blind and I'm stone deaf.' But they still got home in front and, although Aureole was still a horribly difficult ride, a real bond of affection undoubtedly grew between him and Eph Smith. Startled by a suddenly opened umbrella on the way to the start for the King George VI and Queen Elizabeth Stakes, the chestnut whipped round and decanted his rider. Disaster stared them in the face, but, quickly plucking a handful of grass, Smith called, 'Come here, old boy'. The horse walked calmly back and allowed himself to be recaptured. After he had worn down the French colt, Vamos, in a tremendous finish there was nothing particularly calm about his owner. 'As we walked down from the stand,' Bill Curling wrote in his biography of Captain Boyd Rochfort, 'a small figure came racing by.' It was the Queen, running to greet her favourite. Not surprisingly she outdistanced the septuagenarian Captain Moore a good deal more easily than Aureole had beaten Vamos.

That was Aureole's last race and, retired to his owner's Wolverton stud, he began his notable career as a stallion. Even after his departure the 1950s remained a triumphant period for the royal horses. Thanks partly to Carozza – a niece of Sun Chariot bred at the National Stud, who, trained by Noel Murless and ridden by Lester Piggott, won the Oaks – the Queen was again leading owner in 1957. One of her other good winners that year was Doutelle, yet another descendant of Feola, and in 1958 he and the Queen's good filly, Almeria, finished second and third to Ballymoss in the King George VI and Queen Elizabeth Stakes.

The Queen, who had flu at the time, watched this race on

television under the impression that Joe Mercer, who rode Doutelle, had been told to make the pace for Almeria. But to her surprise Almeria set off in front, and it turned out that the two jockeys had been given no special tactical orders. Since Ballymoss was almost certainly the best horse in Europe at the time, it probably made no difference, but the incident and the Queen's slight but undeniable irritation over it demonstrate the close and detailed interest which she takes in every aspect of her horses' lives.

The gallant Doutelle was one of his owner's special favourites and later looked like becoming a very successful stallion when a tragic accident caused his death. Biting the rack-chain by which he was tied up, Doutelle became entangled in it and died while the injuries which he had suffered were being treated. The Queen was deeply upset and later told Lord Porchester that this was the first time since her childhood that a horse had driven her to tears.

Besides caring deeply for her horses' welfare, she has an eagle eye for detail both in the stable and on the gallops, and is also an excellent judge of conformation. This last quality was demonstrated in 1956 when, attending the Doncaster yearling sales with Captain Moore and Lord Porchester, the Queen personally chose two fillies. One of them Stroma, cost only 1,500 guineas and, when mated with Doutelle after her racing career, she produced Canisbay who, to the Queen's delight, won the Eclipse Stakes in 1957. The other filly, Petronella, was later sold, but she too became a successful brood-mare, producing Con Brio and four other winners.

Much of the credit for the great success enjoyed by the royal horses in the 1950s belongs to Captain Charles Moore, stud manager to the Queen and George VI for more than twenty-five years. A tall, handsome, grey-haired Irishman, he ran the royal stud and breeding on strict traditional lines and not without some very definite prejudices. Although understandably devoted to Hyperion and his stock, for instance, he would never use either Fair Trial (because of the traces of American blood in his pedigree) or Nearco (partly because he had been imported from Italy by a bookmaker). Despite these foibles, Moore's great charm easily bridged the gap in age between himself and his chief employer and helped to make her first decade as an owner enjoyable as well as successful. He was also a very considerable judge, and among his many triumphs was the purchase for only 100 guineas of Malapert, whose son, Pall Mall, gave the Queen her first home-bred Classic victory in the 1958 Two Thousand Guineas.

After Captain Moore's retirement in 1960 the royal stud and horses went into one of those low periods which almost all studs suffer from time to time. After a while a committee was formed, consisting of Lord Porchester, Lord Tryon and Peter Burrell, then manager of the National Stud, to devise a new policy in consultation with the Queen. They decided that new blood – and especially more speed – should be brought in. On the death of Richard Shelley who had succeeded Captain Moore, the management of the royal stud was taken over by Michael Oswald. A new position as general racing manager was filled by Lord Porchester, an expert and successful breeder in his own right, and also for many years one of the Queen's greatest friends. With the help of these two men the royal racing establishment has been considerably transformed and has now regained its old momentum. Highclere's successes must have been a particular source of pleasure for Lord Porchester. The filly was named after his father's home near Newbury, and it was on his suggestion that her dam, Highlight, was mated with Queen's Hussar at a surprisingly low 250 guineas, considering that the latter is now famous as the sire of Brigadier Gerard. Queen's Hussar, who belonged to Lord Porchester's father, Lord Carnarvon, was comparatively 'unfashionable' when Highlight visited him, but the mare is almost incestuously inbred to Hyperion, and

Lord Porchester believed, on the principle of 'hybrid vigour', that a complete outcross was worth trying.

When Sir Cecil Boyd Rochfort retired, having saddled the winners of 136 races for the Queen, some of her horses had already been sent to Peter Hastings Bass at Kingsclere in Berkshire. But Hastings Bass was a very sick man, and, when he retired, it was decided to divide the royal string between his successor at Kingsclere, Ian Balding, and Dick Hern at West Ilsley.

These two trainers have a good deal in common. Both are bold and skilful horsemen, who love the excitement of the hunting field, and Ian Balding, a brilliant all-round athlete, was a very successful amateur rider before he took out a trainer's licence. A rugger blue, he twice played full-back for Cambridge and rode a winner over fences on the same day. Both men also have, as Sir Cecil Boyd Rochfort had before them, deep admiration and respect for their principal patron's expert knowledge of racing, breeding and horses in general.

Each spring, a full year in advance, the Queen, in consultation with Lord Porchester and Michael Oswald, plans the matings of her mares. Following the deaths of Doutelle and Aureole, the St Leger winner, Ribero, has stood at her Sandringham stud; and since 1975, when she bought a quarter share in another St Leger winner, Bustino, joint hero with Grundy of that unforgettable King George VI and Queen Elizabeth Stakes, Bustino has been standing at Wolverton. The twenty-three brood-mares in the royal stud are quartered at Sandringham and Wolverton, but the Queen first leased and has now bought another stud at Polhampton in Hampshire, where the foals go when they are weaned. Then as yearlings they are divided equally between Kingsclere and West Ilsley, where the Queen visits them as often as her busy life permits, usually three or four times a year.

The standard of the royal mares has been steadily improved until, as Lord Porchester says with pride, every one of them is either herself the winner of a pattern race, out of such a winner or half-sister to one. It would be foolhardy to predict the fortunes of the horses now in training, but last season at least five two-year-olds, notably Card Player and Fife and Drum, showed unmistakable promise, as did Highclere's half-sister, Circlet. Mr Paul Mellon generously gave the Queen two nominations to Mill Reef and, when that great horse went to stud, they produced two more exciting prospects, a two-year-old out of Albany called English Harbour and a yearling out of Highclere named Milford after Lord Porchester's house.

Although racing, and all that goes with it, is the Queen's favourite hobby and form of relaxation, horses of many different kinds play a part in her life and she in theirs. She has always loved riding for its own sake, not competitively like her daughter but perhaps chiefly because of the chance it gives her, alone or with her family and friends, to forget the constant cares and demands imposed by her position.

The annual Trooping of the Colour on her official birthday is the only occasion on which she rides in public and also the only time she rides sidesaddle although, with characteristic thoroughness, she practises for several weeks each year before the ceremony. She usually rides astride, choosing from several horses, some of them retired from the racecourse, either when she is on holiday at Sandringham and Balmoral or at weekends in Windsor Great Park.

Her first mount at the Trooping (as Princess Elizabeth) was the chestnut police horse, Winston, but several others have carried her since on Horseguards Parade, most often recently the black mare, Burmese, who was a gift from the Royal Canadian Mounted Police.

Nor of course are thoroughbreds by any means the only horses bred in the royal paddocks. Doublet, on whom Princess Anne won the European Three Day Event Championship, was originally bred in an unsuccessful attempt to produce a polo pony for Prince Philip. Like her father and grandfather before her, the Queen also breeds both Fell and Highland ponies and, since the Austrians gave her some Haflingers during a state visit to that country, they too have founded a family. Though perfectly suitable for riding, the Fell ponies are, like their Highland cousins, mostly used for stalking during the royal family's holiday at Balmoral.

Apart from those involved in racing, all the Queen's horses and equine interests are managed by Colonel Sir John Miller, who was partly responsible for introducing Prince Philip to the difficult and hazardous sport of competitive driving when he gave up polo. Sir John has also helped to introduce Prince Charles to the hunting field, and he is of course responsible for all the carriage horses used on the many spectacular ceremonial occasions which are part of the royal year. Most of the famous Windsor greys are now bought in Germany or Holland, but the Queen is also an enthusiastic patron of the Cleveland Bay Society. She owns a Cleveland stallion herself and breeds some of her carriage horses, either pure Clevelands or crossbreeds with Hanoverian or Oldenburg mares.

Taught to ride by Horace Smith and his daughter, Sybil, the Queen gave all her own children their early riding lessons, and there is no need to mention the pride and pleasure she has derived from Princess Anne's rise to world class as a horsewoman.

Even in this mechanical age the horse plays some part in the lives of millions in this country, whether they ride him, breed him, back him or merely watch and enjoy his beauty, courage and agility. So, in Jubilee Year, it would be difficult to exaggerate the good fortune of a horse-loving nation in having a royal family which shares that love in so many different ways.

Princess Anne's skill has entitled her to represent Britain in the Olympic Games. Prince Charles, a keen polo player when his duties permit, is fast becoming an equally keen hunting man. Their grandmother, Queen Elizabeth the Queen Mother, is by far National Hunt racing's most popular owner and, although Prince Philip has hung up his polo boots, he is a bold and fearless coachman. In all these pursuits they are encouraged and supported by the Queen, to whose life, as we have seen, the horse has contributed so much. The twentieth century may be dominated by internal combustion engines, atomic energy and supersonic jets, but in the British royal family the horse still holds a place of honour.

The Case against the Monarchy

ROYAL persons are necessarily divorced from the true opinions of people that count, and are almost always obliged to take safe and commonplace views. To them, clever men are 'prigs'; clever women 'too advanced'; Liberals are 'Socialists'; the uninteresting 'pleasant'; the interesting 'intriguers' and the dreamers 'mad'. But when all is said and done, our King devotes what time he does not spend upon sport and pleasure ungrudgingly to duty.

Autobiography of Margot Asquith, 1922.

... under the guise of keeping up our traditions, we are in danger of preserving rubbish from the past, which no longer has, even if it were conceded that it ever had, any value in the morale-making which is absolutely vital to a great nation; especially a nation in our position when we are coming to the crisis of our fate.

Ramshackledom: A Critical Appraisal of the Establishment,
L. G. Pine, Secker & Warburg, 1962.

IN this Jubilee year of the Queen's accession, it might seem churlish, if not treacherous, to question the worth of the institution of monarchy, and whether it should be allowed to continue to exist either in its present form – or at all.

The monarchy's most devoted admirers are its worst enemies. The claims made by them on its behalf are invariably a mixture of extravagant exaggeration, unprovable assertion, a degree of hoodwinking and mindless devotion.

For twenty-five years HM Queen Elizabeth II has sat on a throne surrounded by a morass of disillusion, decadence and decay. Leading politicians with varying degrees of competence have engaged in deferential, courteous, smiling, hand-kissing sessions with Her Majesty as the ship of state has drifted remorselessly towards the rocks.

In the course of her reign the Queen has seen seven different Prime Ministers come and go. She may see more yet. Whatever advice, warning or encouragement she may have given them, the nation's problems have worsened rather than improved. 'The new Elizabethan era' which was trumpeted in with such absurd romanticism twenty-five years ago has gone sour. The monarchists claim that the institution gives Britain an element of continuity and stability, as if that of itself were good justification for its continued existence. The same argument can be adduced in favour of the House of Lords – the only hereditary legislative Chamber of Parliament left in the world. The continuity of the last quarter century has been the continuity of British decline. Her Majesty cannot be blamed for that. She has been a passive spectator of it, neither inspiration nor hindrance. When Mr Walter Bagehot wrote his authoritative essays on the British constitution 100 years ago, a separate essay was devoted to the monarchy. Speaking of Queen Victoria, Bagehot said, 'Without her in England the present English government would fail and pass away'. That was as much nonsense then as it would be today. In his brilliant introduction to the 1972 reissue of Bagehot's essays, the late R. H. S. Crossman wrote: 'The myths and legends of a Monarchy are only credible to the masses so long as those who propagate them believe their own propaganda. What gives the British Monarchy its unique strength is the fact that the Court, the aristocracy and the Church – not to mention the middle classes – are just as credulous worshippers of it as the masses.'

He might well have added – in his list of 'credulous worshippers' – prominent, self-styled left-wing leaders of the present Labour party, like Sir Harold Wilson, Anthony Wedgwood Benn, the Rt Hon. Michael Foot MP *et al.* Not much comment need be wasted on them, though Sir Harold in particular merits harsh words of censure for the manner in which, over his years as Prime Minister, he fawned needlessly over the monarchy, at the same time never hesitating to use it if he thought it might serve a party political purpose. One recalls his use of the Queen's name to rally the Rhodesian rebels to his side – a worthy cause no doubt, but a completely ineffectual gimmick. More offensive to his own party in particular was Sir Harold's misuse of the honours system, and especially his last list on retirement when he handed out peerages and knighthoods to some very dubious characters and to people who, if not sworn enemies of the Labour movement, were not counted among its best friends.

In these matters too the Queen deserves sympathy rather than blame, though she herself has doled out medals, ribbons and titles to her own family and friends – people with no outstanding merit and of no great use to the nation. In such small ways the Crown is symbolic of much that is wrong in Britain today – what Crossman described as 'reliance on [this kind of] organized deception'.

'*Organized deception*' – that is the case in a nutshell. At best the monarchy is irrelevant to the difficulties we now face. And at worst it behaves, and is allowed to behave, as if we were still living in a world which owed us – and particularly *them* – a living. Even in this Jubilee year the Queen let it be known that she wished celebrations to be on a modest scale, with minimal cost to the ratepayers! How on earth did she think those local jamborees were to be paid for? No local council has a cornucopia like the Duchy of Lancaster or the Duchy of Cornwall to draw on. Every new lick of paint, every new carpet and every bottle of wine or whisky drunk by the guzzling 'guests' has to be paid for – out of the rates. And the £½ million on a new royal train – out of the taxpayers.

Which brings me directly to the cost of the monarchy. It is a matter which can never be dealt with accurately. No one can know the real cost in money terms. It might be possible, for instance, to calculate the total cost of the building, running and maintenance of the royal yacht over the last thirty years. At today's prices it would be something not less than £100 million. Gains which have accrued from the royal vessel – the prestige of overseas visits, the pride in British craftsmanship, and the rest – are incalculable, though one suspects they are marginal. Royal finances are tangled in the cobwebs of history. The story is a mixture of scarcely concealed private royal greed and increasing public expenditure.

Provision from the public purse dates back to the first Civil List Act of 1697, but the modern Civil List, that is, financial provision for the monarch from public funds began in 1760. Seventy years before that, Parliament had agreed to pay an annual £600,000 to William and Mary *for the running of the whole machine of civil government.* The italics are important. In that era the King was responsible for running the whole apparatus of government. He was the head of a landed aristocracy. They secured ownership of their land by theft, confiscation and the use of force. From very early days successive monarchs behaved in true capitalist fashion. Their natural allies were and still are the wealth- and property-owning aristocracy. Right up to the middle of the nineteenth century the royal finances were a skein of mystery and controversy. Corrupt as he was himself, that high priest of Toryism, Edmund Burke, got an Act through Parliament in 1782 to control, if not eliminate, royal avarice, intransigence and corruption.

The 1760 'deal' was the direct outcome of mounting demands for greater public scrutiny of royal spending and the growth of royal debts. It was not magnanimity on the part of the monarchy which led to that 'bargain', but rather its eagerness to get out of the increasingly costly business of running the government machine. The 'surrender' of the revenue from the Crown lands in return for a fixed, steady annual cash payment was about the best deal the monarchy has made these last 200 years. The revenue from the Crown lands is hardly enough to run a big teaching hospital. The cost of government is of mind-boggling magnitude. When the apologists for the Crown assert, as they do, that the state makes a profit out of the deal, they are standing the facts on their head. But the myth is perpetuated at the beginning of each reign, when great play is made of the 'voluntary surrender' of the Crown estate revenues in exchange for Civil List provision. The exercise is a distortion of historical fact that would do credit to the Soviet Union. Today the distortions and falsehood in this matter continue unabated and unashamed. And no member of the royal family has ever uttered a word to dispel them.

The present reign was heralded as the beginning of a glittering new Elizabethan era. In the immediate aftermath of post-war bankruptcy, austerity and rationing the royal cast could not have been chosen better. Truly a Divine hand seemed to have been at work. The leading lady was young, beautiful and modest, with a blond, handsome young husband with salt sea water and royal blood in his veins. The succession had already been secured with the birth of Prince Charles. The Divine hand had been working overtime. The Archbishop of Canterbury naturally gave his fulsome blessing by declaring at the Coronation that the nation was at Holy Communion. Whilst the Poet Laureate, not to be outdone, was penning idle thoughts in verse about the King of Kings who was on our side on this Glorious Day.

But meanwhile there was the question of cash to be decided. For Winston Churchill, the Prime Minister of the day, it was embarrassing that this had to be dealt with by Parliament at all. He bullied the 1952 Civil List Committee into meek acceptance of whatever the royal family demanded. There were few radical souls in the House of Commons to object to the secrecy and extravagance of it all. No evidence given to the Committee was published. Little was given. The money was just doled out – £70,000 a year to the Queen Mother; £35,000 annually to the Duke of Gloucester; £40,000 a year to Prince Philip; £15,000 yearly to Princess Margaret – and a global sum of £475,000 for the Civil List which included a 'salary' element of £60,000 for the Queen herself. The basic old-age pension at that time was less than £100 *a year*.

The proposals went through the House of Commons with scarely a whimper of protest. This victory of the Conservative establishment was complete and overwhelming.

The reign had begun on a firm financial footing. A sum of £70,000 had been set aside each year to take care of the inflation regarded as inevitable. In addition the more important members of the royal family had cast-iron guarantees against the ravages of rising prices and costs – notably the Queen herself and her oldest son Prince Charles. The Queen had access to the tax-free income accruing from the Duchy of Lancaster, her son to the tax-free revenues coming to him from the Duchy of Cornwall.

The Queen had taken £110,000 from the Duchy of Lancaster in 1952. In the ensuing years up to and including 1976 she has taken £4½ *million*.

In the same period her son, Prince Charles, has garnered £3 *million*, the last year's gathering bringing a paltry £145,000. A lean year unlikely to be repeated.

There is still a degree of confusion about which taxes are paid by members of the royal family. The original theory was that, as tax revenue accrues nominally at least to the Crown, the monarch cannot pay taxes to himself or herself. This theory has been eroded over the years but still applies in substantial part. In its memorandum to the 1972 Select Committee on the Civil List the Treasury asserted: 'As part of the Royal Prerogative, the Queen is not liable to pay tax unless Parliament says so, either explicitly or by inevitable inference.

There is no distinction for this purpose between the private and public aspects of the Sovereign.'

The present situation applies so far as was revealed to that 1972 Committee: the Queen pays no income tax either on the Civil List or on the income from the Duchy of Lancaster.

The Crown Private Estate Act of 1862 has been so interpreted as to ensure that the Sovereign pays only rates on her private estates of Sandringham and Balmoral. She does *not* pay tax on the substantial farm profits. And she is entitled to claim refund on any income tax deducted at source, for example, on company dividends. Nobody may know whether she does claim such refunds. It would be interesting to know. The information has been refused.

Prince Charles does not pay tax on what he takes from the Duchy of Cornwall. This fabulous concession and privilege dates back to an opinion given by the law officers of the Crown in 1913. At that time the radical Chancellor of the Exchequer, the Liberal Lloyd George, was seeking to tax land values, which would have fallen heavily on the Duchy of Cornwall. The Duchy officials had then apparently appealed to the law officers for a ruling and it is that ruling which still applies today. It makes very strange reading. It is not surprising that over the years it had been kept a closely guarded secret. Only by chance did it come into my hands a year or two ago. In evidence to the 1972 Select Committee the Inland Revenue were completely unable to explain what the 1913 law officers meant when referring to the 'peculiar title of the Prince of Wales to the Duchy of Cornwall'.

The subject had been returned to again in 1921, when the law officers of the Crown were asked for their opinion on the specific matter of income-tax liability of the Duchy revenue. These officers reaffirmed the 1913 opinion, again without giving reasons for it. That the successor to the throne should be receiving such an enormous unearned income is bad enough. That he should be receiving it tax free, that he should be enjoying such a privilege based on a legal opinion given sixty years ago which could not stand up in a court of law is as offensive as it is indefensible. It is no justification to say that in lieu of tax Prince Charles 'voluntarily surrenders' half his entitlement to the revenues of the Duchy. The best example he could set the British people in this matter would be to agree that his income should be taxed in exactly the same way as is the income of every other citizen of the land. And in the event of his failure to do that, some government and some Chancellor should have the courage to put the matter right – and soon.

But the tax privilege does not end with exemption from income tax. The Crown is exempt from paying death duties. That exemption applies to *all* estates, including Balmoral and Sandringham. Nor is the Queen liable to capital gains tax – or capital transfer tax. The latter tax was the subject of correspondence between myself and the Treasury in October 1976. The Queen had bought a mansion for her daughter Princess Anne. The price paid was reported to be £500,000. The Press was interested. Had the Queen paid capital transfer tax? Had she volunteered to pay it? Had the Treasury pressed her to pay? The questions were put to the Palace, and to the Treasury. No answer was forthcoming. It was a private matter, they said. These are *not* private matters. They are questions of public interest and concern. To remain silent about them is to encourage the worst suspicions.

That the Queen is one of the wealthiest people in the world there can be no doubt. That wealth has been accumulated by a combination of shrewdness and sound business advice from city gentlemen, but above all by priceless tax privileges not available to any of her subjects. The fact that for over eighty years the royal fortunes, including that accruing to the 'owner' of the Duchy of Cornwall, have escaped the ravages of estate duty must have put hundreds of millions of pounds into the royal coffers. What on earth do they do with it all?

Some of these questions were put when the new Select Committee on the Civil List was established in 1971–2. The questions were asked. But few were answered. HM the Queen flatly refused to reveal the size of her private fortune. *Repeated* refusals were made. It was a measure of the strength of the hold which she must have felt she had on the government of the day and on the minds and affections of the public. The refusal was a constitutional outrage. But what little adverse comment was made by the media was not sustained for long.

That Committee did indeed break new ground. After some dispute, it was agreed that all the evidence should be recorded; and that it should all be published. To the great distaste of the Conservative members.

For the first time the Treasury and the Inland Revenue gave written and oral evidence on the tax liability of individual members of the royal family.

For the first time, minority reports were presented and published, one written by myself, the other by the Rt Hon. Douglas Houghton. Both were rejected by the Committee, voting largely on party lines, and the report finally accepted was that produced by the Tory Chancellor of the Exchequer, the Rt Hon. Anthony Barber. It gave the royal family virtually everything they had asked for.

But the public exposure, limited though it had been, had proved to be too much. Steps were taken to prevent such an inquiry from ever happening again. There will be no more interrogatory, investigatory House of Commons Select Committees to pry into the royal finances. The books were shut tighter than ever before. There will be no more Civil List Acts of Parliament, with all the accompanying adverse and distasteful publicity. The victory for the monarchy appears to be complete and comprehensive. From now on they will get their increased endowments without parliamentary and Press inquisition. The shutters were down on the royal finances. Buckingham Palace was as secure as the Kremlin. Open government stops at its gates.

So what is to be done? We must await a government with the will to act. For a start such a government could take over the so-called private estates of the Duchies of Lancaster and Cornwall. The state could take complete control of the Grace and Favour residences – about 140 of them, currently a perk in the gift of the Queen – with the tenants, including Princess Margaret, ex royal private secretaries and other royal family favourites paying a full economic rent. At present they pay *no rent*.

All this property – the two Duchies, the Crown estate, and the Grace and Favour residences – could be amalgamated into one big public estate, managed by Public Estates Commissioners appointed by the Treasury and accountable to Parliament.

Many people of a conservative mind might fear that such fundamental changes would signify the beginning of the end of the monarchy as we know it today. They would be right. The next step could be that proposed by the Labour party during those debates in the House of Commons on the royal finances in 1972, namely the creation of a Department of the Crown. The idea was the brain-child of the Rt Hon. Douglas Houghton, MP – now Lord Houghton – a respectable, royalist, moderate Privy Councillor, who had held high office in the Labour government of the mid-1960s, including a period as Chancellor of the Duchy of Lancaster. Houghton is a great radical traditionalist. He recognized the Crown as 'an integral part of the constitution of the state'. He was motivated by no desire to threaten its status. On the contrary he wanted to ensure its continued existence – by giving it a dust down, by bringing it into the twenty-first century. In his view the time had come 'to separate the financial provisions for the Queen's person from the expenses of the Crown as an institution'.

The proposal was simple and moderate. The royal household was to be reconstituted as a department of state, like the Departments of Education or Agriculture. The main problem was the lack of a ministerial head, plus the different status of the staff. These difficulties are not insurmountable. The royal household could have a status similar to that of the departments of the House of Commons. The Commons is not staffed by civil servants. They are not answerable to government ministers. They are controlled by a body of commissioners, appointed by the House. The Chancellor of the Exchequer is one such commissioner. However, the Commons staff are recruited through the civil-service machinery and are paid and pensioned under terms similar to those enjoyed by civil servants.

In a similar way the royal household departments could be placed under the control of a standing Crown Commission, appointed in the usual way by royal warrant. A minister of the government of the day could be appointed to the Commission, thus preserving a direct link with Parliament. The Lord Chamberlain, or a successor with a less traditional title, could be the chairman. This Crown Commission would thus have its own special status with its own special relationship to Parliament and at the same time have a close connection with the Sovereign.

The Crown Commission would derive its finances from money or monies provided by Parliament through an ordinary vote which would be published annually along with the votes for the other government departments.

On that basis the staff would not be civil servants, but would be treated as if they were in matters of pay and pensions. The Queen's immediate personal attendants and advisers, such as private secretary, could be excluded from these arrangements and paid directly by the Queen from her personal resources as private employees.

Mr Houghton drew up a chart illustrating the structure he had in mind. He felt it would be necessary to establish ministerial responsibility for the new vote and assumed that this would fall either to the Prime Minister or to the Chancellor of the Exchequer. It would be necessary, too, to appoint a suitable official of the Commission as accounting officer. Other details, such as the power of the House of Commons to scrutinize the detailed royal expenditure, the question of audit and other matters, need not be dealt with here.

In the event the Select Committee on the Civil List had a discussion on the merits of Mr Houghton's ideas and they were rejected by only one vote; the then Liberal party leader Mr Jeremy Thorpe and Mr Harold Wilson both supported the Houghton proposals. One prominent Conservative member of the Committee voted *against* Mr Houghton only when he learned that the Queen herself was opposed to the idea of a Crown Department and the public scrutiny which would inevitably follow. Monarchy does not like public scrutiny. It prefers the cloak of secrecy, which helps to ensure its survival.

However, the matter was pursued on the floor of the House of Commons on 14 December 1971 and again when I myself sought to introduce a Bill to establish a Crown Department of State (4 March 1975). I was supported by 174 members on that occasion, but 207 voted the other way.

There is a massive public opinion against the royal 'hangers-on' – those who hang on to the skirts of the Queen and who for far too long have done too well out of the business of monarchy. High on that list come the two Princesses, Margaret and Anne. They could surely be pensioned off. The Queen herself could decide how to reward her own immediate family out of her own ample private resources. None of them should be any longer a burden on the Exchequer. If they wished to remain as servants of the Crown on the public payroll, they should be paid suitable taxable civil-service rates of pay and come within the ambit of the Crown Department's vote.

Prince Charles might receive special treatment. He might be paid a taxable annual salary equal to that of the Prime Minister.

To summarize the case against the continued existence of the monarchy. The holding of any office by hereditary title will not be tolerated much longer. Especially among the young, long-established and revered institutions are increasingly being challenged and questioned. The church, the civil service, the House of Lords, the monarchy, the City, Parliament itself, are being subject to critical and cynical scrutiny. The United Kingdom as an entity is in the process of disintegration, and the Commonwealth is little more than a romantic hangover of an historical era now ended for ever.

Today the monarchy buttresses and underpins a deferential, class-conscious, divided nation, which has lost its way in the world. As we wallow in our own dreams, clinging to memories of our romantic past, the rest of the world passes us by.

Our 'dignified monarchy will pull us through,' they say. But what dignity is there in the rudeness of the Queen's daughter, Princess Anne? Or in the wayward behaviour of her aunt, Princess Margaret? What was dignified in the career of Mr Angus Ogilvy as a director of Lonrho? Or even in some of the globe-trotting and hectoring speeches of the Queen's Consort, Prince Philip? The moral and spiritual leadership which the Crown is supposed to give us all is almost non-existent. Morally and spiritually Britain is leaderless and declining rapidly. In the process of decay the monarchy is a baneful influence, interested only in its own survival and that of the class system on which it depends.

The heir to the throne waits anxiously in the wings. For twenty years, and possibly more, depending on the longevity of the Queen, Prince Charles, with the help of a multiplicity of advisers, will have to find himself a role as the next principal actor on the royal stage. It cannot be easy to play a 'bit part' for so long. His every move is watched with uncritical adulation by the media and the masses. Every young lady his eye may chance upon is at once put under the closest scrutiny. In the weeks preceding the visit to Britain of the international bailiffs called the International Monetary Fund, British papers were splashed with headlines and pictures about the Prince's impending departure from the Royal Navy. It was a splendid distraction from the brutal reality of our economic bankruptcy, the facts about which must now be told.

Taking as our starting point the Coronation of 2 June 1953, how has the new Elizabethan era worked out? The United Kingdom is a trading nation. 'We must export or die' is a theme never far from the lips or minds of politicians and statesmen. And the Crown, we are told, is good for trade. In 1952 the UK percentage of the total value of world exports was 9. By 1976 that had dropped to 5·6 per cent. In the same period the Republic of West Germany had increased its share of world exports from 5 per cent in 1952 to 11·5 per cent in 1976. The French Republic's share had gone up from 4·8 per cent to 6·7 per cent, and Japan's from 1·6 per cent to 7·1 per cent. Even Italy more than doubled her share of world exports in those last twenty-five years.

The story of Commonwealth trade is equally dismal. The royalist case is most fervently upheld as far as Australia, New Zealand and Canada (the old white Commonwealth) are concerned. But these sentiments are not reflecetd in the trade figures. In 1950 nigh on two-fifths of Australia's total exports came to Britain. Today the figure is less than half what it was. The same pattern is broadly true for New Zealand. Canadian exports have gone down to about a third of what they were in 1950 in percentage terms. In 1950 those three great countries imported large volumes of goods from the UK. Over 50 per cent of Australia's imports in 1950 were from the UK.

Twenty-five years later that was down to about 15 per cent. Sixty per cent of New Zealand's imports were from the UK in 1950. In 1975 the figure was in the region of 18 per cent – less than half.

Desperately the royalists assert that the royal razzamatazz is good for tourism. The Japs and the Germans, the Yanks and the Frenchmen all come here to gape and marvel at our quaint Beefeaters, our royal knights of Windsor, our expensive royal palaces and the street musicians that go with them. What are the facts? The number of visitors to the UK has remained virtually static over the last twenty-five years at between 7 and 8 million. In the same period the number of visitors to Republican USA shot up from 3·2 million in 1952 to 14·1 million in 1974; in Republican France from 3·2 million to 9·8 million; in Republican Italy from 4·1 million to 12·4 million, and in Spain from 1·5 million to 19·5 million. The figures are not entirely reliable or strictly comparable. They are derived from the UN Statistical Year Book and from International Travel Statistics. Whatever else they prove, they demonstrate that the tourist trade has expanded far more dramatically in the USA, Germany, Italy, France and Spain than it has in the UK and that it has nothing to do with the fact that we happen to be saddled with a monarchy.

If we try to use statistics to measure international standards of living, the same dismal story repeats itself. By any yardstick the UK has fallen behind in the race.

Since 1952 the UK annual growth rate has been 4·8 per cent, up to 1975. In the USA, West Germany, France, Italy, Japan, Sweden and Denmark the comparable figures were 5·6, 9·1, 8·8, 8·6, 16, 6·9 and 7·1.

Finally, a purely internal UK yardstick. In 1952 the average monthly number unemployed was 361,500 or 1·7 per cent of the total work force. In October 1976 the figures were 1,305,000 and 5·5 per cent respectively.

These statistics are paraded not to debunk any pro-royalist

cause, nor in any sense to gloat over the miserable performance of post-war Britain. The Queen and the institution
which she and her family so modestly represent are in no way
to blame directly for this depressing story. But, if they are not
to blame, they can hardly be praised either. Their apologists
may claim that but for our royal family the record might have
been worse. If so, it is not a very attractive prospectus on
which to embark into the twenty-first century.

Such facts and figures as can be assembled point remorselessly to the costly irrelevance of monarchy. The best that can
be said of it is that we could get something conceivably worse,
and more costly. And in any event, in some unquantifiable
way, our monarchy makes us all *feel* good. There we have a
shining light, dazzling us all with its pristine beauty. Petty
politicians might squabble in the gutters of democracy; they
come and they go, but the Crown rides beyond the ruck,
above the feuding of the common herd. Labour party leaders
are corrupted into mouthing and possibly believing that the
monarchy is non-party-political, that it transcends the economic and social struggles in which we are *all* engaged. I refute
such talk as gobbledegook.

In the last year or two siren voices have been heard about
the increasing threats to our personal freedoms. Lord Hailsham and others are fond of rolling out their tumbrils whenever a socialist government gets power. In 1945, immediately
after the break up of the wartime coalition government, Winston Churchill, as he then was, turned on the hitherto acceptable socialist members of his wartime government and
sought to chill the blood of the electors by the prospect of a
Gestapo, a secret police, with the advent of a Labour government. Fortunately the electorate was more mature than Mr
Churchill had imagined. Between 1945 and 1950 Britain wit-
nessed the greatest social revolution in its history, brought
about through the ballot box and Parliamentary democracy.
The Crown was on the side of Churchill and the capitalist

system for which he spoke. For capitalism and the Tory party the monarchy is invaluable. It is an integral part of the economic and social order in which they believe. No member of the royal family has ever believed in, or actually espoused, the ideals of left-wing politicians. By birth, upbringing, education and training they are taught, and must be taught, that they were born to reign if not to rule. The educational system is so designed as not to challenge these concepts. Who ever saw in a school or university history textbook anything critical of the monarchy? Point to one royal child who has ever been educated within the public system. They opt out of the unequal struggle in which 95 per cent of our children have to survive. The royal children's parents make their political decisions in education as in other matters. And they act like any other wealthy Tory parents. Under the specious guise of freedom of choice they use their inherited, untaxed wealth to *buy* privileged private education. They are entitled to do that so long as a private, privileged sector of education remains. What they are not entitled to do is, having used their unearned and unmerited wealth to buy education denied to the great masses of our children, to pose as the champions of those masses. They are not entitled to claim that they even understand, still less sympathize with, the hopes and aspirations of the tens of millions of our people who have to go through life suffering and struggling socially and economically in a system which is encapsulated by the royal family.

It is not surprising that Prince Philip joins the hunt along with Lord Hailsham – and before them Churchill – in their dire warnings about the mythical threats to personal freedom. It's not surprising, either, that a Royal should marry City wealth in the person of Angus Ogilvy, who was mixed up with the unsavoury Lonrho affair. He got out pretty quickly when the sordid truth began to be revealed. But the capitalist system and the rich pickings that come from it are still dear to the heart and no word of public disapproval came from the royal family.

Far from being apolitical, the monarchy is part of the established order of things. It is conservative and Conservative. It is a barrier against change, or against *too radical* changes in our society. A radical monarch is a contradiction in terms. The monarchy is regarded as a staunch ally by reactionary, right-wing elements in our society precisely because it is conservative and reactionary. The same Lord Hailsham who made the absurd claim – in 1947 – that the very existence of our monarchy saved us from tyranny in 1940, and that the absence of one in France caused the French downfall, makes the equally dotty charge that individual freedom is imperilled by a socialist government in 1977. Surely Hailsham must know that the ministers of that government are Her Majesty's ministers. None more royalist than they. And, in any event, how often have we been told, by Hailsham and others, that the Crown is the ultimate safeguard of all our freedoms? Despite the historical *fact* that those freedoms had to be fought for, *against* the Crown and against the landed aristocracy, who were, and still are, natural allies; the theory of the Divine Right of Kings is still far from dead in the minds of many Dukes and dockers, miners and Marquises.

The same voices which shrilly proclaim that our liberties are in danger also assert that the Crown is the ultimate safeguard of our individual rights, the last bastion against dictatorship. Is the day just round the corner, then, when the monarch will have to defend the people against the dictatorial advances of *Her* government? If so, how and when will the crunch come? And how credible would the monarchy be in any such conceivable set of circumstances?

Either the Hailshams are serious or they are not. If serious, they should take comfort under the protective wing of the

Crown. If not, they expose themselves as political opportunists and charlatans.

Moreover in the event of the threat of possible dictatorship, an elected President, representing *all* the people, would be a surer guardian of individual freedom than would an extremely wealthy, unrepresentative, upper-class family, who hold position by heredity, with no claim to any distinction whatsoever.

No one should be afraid of upholding the principles of democratic election of our leaders. Public accountability must extend upwards and downwards. The UK today is one of the most centralized nation states in the modern democratic world. Powers of decision-making are too much concentrated in London and Whitehall. And too many decisions affecting the lives of ordinary men and women are taken by urepresentative, faceless and unaccountable, unelected men and women. We may never be certain how influential the monarch has been, is or will be in these matters.

If the monarch is as powerless as is sometimes claimed, then why not have such a figurehead elected – by universal suffrage? If on the other hand the head of state still has residual powers, in theory if not in practice, why shouldn't he or she be accountable to the people for the manner in which such powers are exercised?

For my part, the case for a democratically elected head of state, a President, is unanswerable. The case for the continued existence of an hereditary monarchy is as weak and indefensible as that for retaining a predominantly hereditary House of Lords. It is a hangover from feudal times. It serves no useful purpose. To those who want to see fundamental changes in the nature of our society, it is an impediment which must be abolished.

The transition from monarchy to presidency need not be painful. The first steps along that path have already been indicated earlier in this essay. A future government could make it clear that this march towards a Republic would be completed by the end of the century. And when the process has been completed, we shall soon begin to wonder why we ever put up with the monarchy for so long. There is a deep yearning for fundamental changes in our constitution. We have been satisfied with cosmetic surgery for far too long.

The Case for the Monarchy

IF the test of a democratic institution today is the extent to which it is popular, egalitarian and capable of eliciting the active participation of ordinary people, then the contemporary British monarchy must be given high marks. About the first of these criteria – its popularity – there is surely no question. All the polls, and everyday experience as well, affirm it. No other institution to do with the governance of Britain enjoys more public support – not government, not Parliament, not the civil service, not the Press, not the City of London, or the Bank of England, not the Church of England, not the BBC, not even the Royal Navy or the police, all of which are currently felt to be functioning less well than they should; less well than they did. Only the monarchy has survived the decline of Britain during the last quarter of a century with its prestige wholly untarnished, perhaps even enhanced, as much abroad as at home.

When a British Prime Minister travels overseas, or a British tycoon, or a British admiral, they all cut sad figures, so humiliating is the contrast between the old days and the new. But this is not so with the Queen. The respect and admiration which everything British used to inspire throughout the world is now evoked only by the monarchy, which is still an object of unique and universal admiration. In strict terms of consumer choice, so to speak, the monarchy comes tops. So much is incontrovertible, too obvious to require emphasis.

But in what sense is the monarchy egalitarian? Here we

get into deeper and rather choppier waters of controversy, since it is often argued by the left that the monarchy shores up the old class system by lending some of its own glamour to the aristocracy, which shines in its reflected glory. At first glance, there would seem to be some truth in this contention, since those closest to the royal family do tend to be the ancient families: Cecils, Howards, Cavendishes and such like. Certainly the Court is largely made up of noble names.

But is this really important? Does the fact that the Duchess of This or That is the Lady of the Bedchamber, or that Lord So and So is Gold Stick extraordinary, or that the Marquis X or Y is Lord Chamberlain, or that Earl Such and Such is Master of the Horse, significantly buttress the power of the ancient nobility? Are those graciously allowed to expend a small fortune on putting the Queen up in their great private mansions really privileged? This line of attack on the monarchy – that it gives support and comfort to a hereditary ruling class – is surely rather far-fetched, since the spectacle of what was once a genuinely ruling class reduced to such purely honorific functions, far from enhancing its dignity, tends to underline the extent of its decline. For the courtier is the most servile of creatures, compelled to behave with a degree of conspicuous humility which would be tolerated by no other walk of contemporary British life. Close association with the royal family does the very opposite of puff people up with pride, since no other group in the kingdom is expected to accept such a condition of crawling subjection.

It is in this sense that the monarchy is, and always has been, an egalitarian institution, cutting the mighty down to size, since in its presence all classes – the Duke quite as much as the dustman – are equally compelled to bow their head and bend their knee.

I recall, as a young man, being present on an occasion, shortly after Queen Elizabeth II's accession, when Winston Churchill paid his homage to the new sovereign. Winston

Churchill at the time was the most illustrious figure in the world, than whom nobody was greater or more glorious. Yet he approached this mere slip of a girl in a posture of deep awe, respect and reverence. The humblest in the land could not have displayed a mien of more abject deference. The monarchy is a great leveller, since from the lofty peak of its pre-eminence all other ranks appear equally negligible.

Richard Crossman finally grasped this truth, as is clear from the second volume of his memoirs, where he writes: 'I remember once asking Godfrey Agnew (then the Queen's Private Secretary) whether she preferred the Tories to us because they were our social superiors and he said, "I don't think so. The Queen doesn't make fine distinctions between politicians of different parties. They all roughly belong to the same social category in her view." I think that's true,' concluded Crossman. Of course it is true. The one person least likely to be snobbish is the Queen herself.

This same point was brought home very forcibly to me by another meeting with royalty, many years later, when the Queen and Prince Philip visited the offices of the *Telegraph* in Fleet Street. As soon as they entered the building, all members of the staff, from the proprietor downwards were reduced to the same condition of awed servility, the editors no less than the messenger boys, to each of whom the royal personages displayed an identical expression of courteous condescension, making no distinctions between the various ranks of the hierarchy.

When they attended the editor's conference, his nervousness was quite as great as that of the young reporter, since the gap in status between royalty and its subjects is so much wider than the gap between subject and subject. The royal presence temporarily obliterated all social and professional distinctions, since everybody was aware that as subjects of the Queen they were much closer to each other, had much more in common with each other, than with their Sovereign who towered above them all.

As a result the visit of the Queen was an exceptionally egalitarian experience, rather in the same way as a church service, since, just as all worshippers are equal in the eyes of God, so are all subjects equal in the eyes of royalty. After she had gone, senior executives could be seen comparing notes with their secretaries as to what she had said, laughing and joking together in shared relief at having gone through an ordeal without mishap. Absurd as it may seem, one was reminded of those stories of how officers and men in the First World War were brought into communion for the first time by the ordeal of battle, the shared danger of death forging a common bond between different classes.

No one genuinely concerned with the ideal of equality should underestimate the relevance of monarchy to its realization, as much, if not more so, in a democratic age as in any other. For it is the essence of monarchy that all ranks hold it in equal awe, are equally its servants, and this applies to the great figures of the democracy as well as the great figures of the aristocracy or the plutocracy or the theocracy. Precisely because it is an institution resting on a principle or concept separate from, and superior to, the sources of all other forms of secular power, it can and does subdue every form of pride and arrogance: the pride and arrogance of elected power as much as the pride and arrogance of wealth or the pride and arrogance of lineage, or even the pride and arrogance of churches. The democracy, the bureaucracy, the aristocracy, the plutocracy, the theocracy, all approach the monarchy from a shared posture of subjection. The Prime Minister, the head of the civil service, the Earl Marshal, the chairman of the largest corporation, the governor of the Bank of England, the archbishop all bow before the throne, as low as the meanest, poorest, humblest in the land.

Only one small group, in present circumstances, refuses to

do so, or complains about doing so, and these are the socialist ideologues of the Labour party. But they are the exception which proves the rule, since in a democracy the only really significant and substantial form of pride and arrogance is bound to come from that quarter. No aristocrat or tycoon or prelate finds it undignified or humiliating to bow before the throne, since their power today is not of the prideful kind. In a democracy it is only a certain type of popular representative who might be tempted to feel himself too grand to bend his knee in the presence of his Sovereign, rather as *some* great aristocrats and *some* great bishops and *some* great magnates did in the olden days.

Let me refer again here to the Crossman diaries, which are extremely revealing in this respect, since they contain the author's repeated moans and groans against the convention which requires busy Cabinet ministers to travel, sometimes all the way to Balmoral in Scotland, for meetings of the Privy Council. Crossman, who was Lord President of the Council at the time, took the view that it should be the Queen who came to him rather than he to her. To his mind there was something very *infra dig.* about important ministers being expected to dance attendance on someone whom he clearly regarded as a mere anachronism.

To my mind, however, the proper reaction of a genuinely egalitarian minister would have been to welcome this opportunity for self-abasement. Instead of resenting the indignity, a true democrat might be expected to recognize the point of the exercise, and to understand that in modern circumstances, where democracy reigns supreme, such affronts to ministerial pride are thoroughly desirable. For under a democratic system it is surely ministerial rather than royal arrogance that most needs to be humbled.

This is not a political or a constitutional question, since the Queen has no power to impose her will in these matters. If Crossman had wished to defy the convention and insist on the Queen travelling to him, rather than the other way round, she would have had to give way. But he lacked the courage to do so, not because she would chop his head off, but because public opinion would have regarded such behaviour as ill-mannered and loutish. In other words, although he liked to suppose that his resentment was inspired by concern for egalitarian and democratic principles, it was really nothing more respectable than wilful pride in ministerial rank.

Much the same can be said about a socialist minister like the late Anthony Crosland, who refused to dress up in a white tie for ceremonial occasions at Buckingham Palace. In theory he was supposedly striking a blow at the class system and championing the cause of the ordinary people by disdaining to don the uniform of the nobs. But of course the great majority of ordinary people would give their eye teeth to take a day off work and travel up to see the Queen at Balmoral. In resenting these royal conventions, socialist ministers are not putting themselves on the level of the people. They are putting themselves above the people, championing principles which are in no genuine sense democratic or egalitarian. Their attitude is profoundly elitist, rooted in feelings of social superiority – in fact, inegalitarian and undemocratic – and in so far as the monarchy is still strong enough to frustrate these forms of ministerial disrespect it is because it has the support of the people in doing so.

In the event, Crossman did go on travelling up to Balmoral, and even began to see the point of this ritual, just as Mr Crosland – under pressure from prudent Mr Callaghan – let it be known that in future he would dress properly for palace ceremonials. Small concessions of course, too small doubtless to be thought worth mentioning in the constitutional textbooks. But constitutional textbooks written by academics are notorious for missing the reality of politics. To my mind, the fact that it is almost always the most personally arrogant, bullying and strong-willed of socialist ministers – men like

Crossman and Crosland, or Benn and Foot – who find these royal conventions most difficult to stomach tells us more about the real value of the contemporary monarchy than any amount of high-flown constitutional theory, since it is from exactly that type of very superior person – the modern equivalent of the late Lord Curzon – that the contemporary threat to democracy is likely to come.

The arrogance of a great nobleman has long since ceased to be a public danger, because the principle which fed it – the idea of aristocracy – is no longer in fashion. An aristocrat may be individually arrogant, but this constitutes no political problem, since such a man is cut off from the realities of power. But arrogant ministers are another matter, since only they can feed their individual pride with the sustenance of a reigning doctrine, which at once fortifies and justifies their will to power. In theory, of course, such socialist Lord Curzons can be cut down to size by the votes of the people, or humiliated by parliamentary defeat. But in practice it has to be recognized that the curb to their pride which cuts deepest and which they find most difficult to bear – judging by their memoirs – is that which involves heeding the public's insistence that they be polite to, and put themselves out for, a horsey, non-intellectual, middle-aged woman, whom in other circumstances they would undoubtedly either snub or ignore.

These are not questions of theory, since no abstract construct of a democratic policy would include such an anomalous check on ministerial arrogance. But it is impossible to read the memoirs of democratic ministers without realizing that their relationship with the Crown does constitute a check which is recognizably true to the spirit, if not the theory, of democracy.

Again one comes back to the Crossman diaries, since few other documents take one so close to the reality of democratic politics. What one is compelled to notice on almost every page is its tone of insufferable patronage *de haut en bas* adopted towards 'the people', who appear always as objects to be addressed, manipulated, flattered, bought, deceived, told the truth, as occasion demands. By no stretch of the imagination could the tone be described as one of respect or equality. Nor is this peculiar to Crossman. Democratic rulers may sometimes disguise their contempt for the people more than Crossman bothered to do. But that is a matter merely of differing degrees of discretion. Basically the same patronizing attitude is always more or less apparent. The people are there to be cajoled, harangued, persuaded, talked down to or, as a special treat, taken into one's ministerial confidence.

Needless to say, this is not the ministerial attitude to the particular sections of the people who wield power and authority – the various interest groups and so on. To these the ministerial approach is quite different, much more equal. But for 'the people', who are theoretically sovereign, ministers feel at best responsibility and at worst exasperation bordering on contempt; most often a bit of both.

But rulers cannot be expected to respect the ruled; never have and never will. The only difference that democracy makes is to induce more ministerial hypocrisy, more dissimulation in public, which may or may not be an improvement. What the monarchy does, however, is to turn the tables on the haughtiness of democratic rulers, since the monarchy is not an abstraction, like 'the people', to be deified in theory but patronized in practice, but a flesh-and-blood person who has to be deified in practice while being patronized in theory. In democratic theory 'the people' are supreme, and the monarchy a mere anomaly. But, in democratic practice, it is the other way round, since royal flesh and blood carries more weight than hot air.

This is not an easy point to make, since it is about the psychology of politicians rather than the theory of politics. My suggestion is that, when a Prime Minister has his weekly audience with the Queen, this is an engagement which symbolizes the essence of democracy more truly in some ways than does his weekly question time in the House of Commons or his public speeches, since the Queen is the one ordinary person in the country – ordinary in the sense of not being a member of the meritocracy or the power elite – to whom he talks without condescension, with whom his relationship is genuinely that of humility, as it is meant to be with 'the people', but in fact never is and never can be.

For the Queen, in our democracy, has come to play the role, act out the part, of 'the sovereign people', combining in her physical person the very contradictory characteristics of that grandiose abstraction, being some*body* who is at once very important and yet strangely impotent, very impressive and yet really rather insignificant, very grand and yet at the same time pathetically weak: the embodiment of those baffling combinations which lie at the heart of the democratic paradox where 'the people' both rule and are ruled, or, in a word, reign – which is what the Queen does.

In other words, strange as it may seem, the Queen and 'the people' have a great deal in common in a democracy, much more in common in practice than do 'the people' and the government, since her role and theirs are equally ceremonial, equally rhetorical, equally meaningless in the real world of power, while at the same time representing moral forces which the real world of power knows it cannot ignore. It is their reluctant recognition of this truth which brings disrespectful ministers into line, compels them to fear the Crown, since in these respects the monarchy is almost the reverse of what Walter Bagehot, in his famous essay, suggested. It is not, as he argued, the ceremonial arm of government but the ceremonial arm of the governed; not so much the visible part of government, useful because it most easily impresses the ruled, as the most visible part of the governed, useful because it most easily impresses the rulers. As the true nature of the democratic system becomes clearer, it is Parliament which is increasingly seen as the ceremonial façade of the constitution – a mere charade – deflecting attention from the true nature of executive power, and the monarchy as the much more genuinely effective popular institution with a democratic role to play which could yet prove very far from make-believe.

Popular, unquestionably *yes*; democratic and egalitarian, also yes. But how does one justify the other criterion mentioned earlier: that the monarchy is an institution capable of eliciting the active participation of the people? At the most obvious level, of course, this is manifestly the case, since the crowds never fail to turn up to participate in royal occasions. To some extent this is obviously their liking for pageantry. But in my opinion it is much more than that; much more than a form of open air free entertainment. It is also a form of political participation, or participation in the governance of the country, a demonstration of popular sovereignty in action.

If anybody doubts this, let him stand in the streets of London just before a royal occasion is due to begin. Who is doing whom a favour: the Queen by deigning to pass by or the crowds by deigning to turn out? Who is most dependent on whom: the crowds on the appearance of the Queen or the Queen on the appearance of the crowds? Of course the crowds would be deeply disappointed if the Queen failed to arrive. But, if the crowds did not arrive, the Queen would be more than disappointed, because they are vitally necessary to her – without them the monarchy would lose its *raison d'être*. In the deepest sense, it is the crowds who are doing her a favour, and she who is dependent on them. And they know this, and so does she. What purports to be a demonstration of public obeisance and loyalty to her is also an exercise of popular patronage *of* her, the mask of love and devotion disguising what is also the face of power.

The pleasure given to the crowds by a royal occasion lies

in the fact that they, ordinary people, are an essential element in its success – almost *the* essential element, since without their enthusiastic cooperation such occasions would be the most dismal flops. In other words they, the people, by agreeing to participate in what are the grandest of state occasions, ennoble themselves, flatter themselves, become at least temporarily an essential part of the grandeur. But the pleasure is enhanced by the knowledge that this grandeur is really theirs since it is generated by, and dependent on, their willingness to believe in it, their acclaim, their cheers. Thus it is that what seems to be an act of popular submission becomes an act of popular affirmation, which is why any diminution in the glory and splendour of these occasions is so opposed by the people, since it is quite as much their glory and their splendour as the Queen's.

In a sense, of course, this is also true of the relationship between democratic politicians and the people, with the former dependent on the latter for their votes. In theory, one might suppose that the act of voting was a much more profound form of participation and a much more real form of power than the act of granting or withdrawing allegiance to the Crown. But, in practice, this may not be the case. My hunch is that when people sing 'God save the Queen', or cheer her in the streets, they feel themselves to be participating in the governance of Britain in a more deep, direct and personal way than when they cast their ballot. For, whereas party politics is essentially a game played by a few, popular acclamation for the monarchy is genuinely democratic in the purest sense, since it is the only form of public life wherein all are equal and none superior or inferior. Because the relationship between the people and the crown is of the heart and not of the head, it is open to all, regardless of age, rank, education, strength of will or wealth. Mass democracy is a phrase, a theory, devoid of real content. The people do not really control the government, except in name. But they do control the monarchy, since without their love it could not exist. Over the monarchy ordinary people are truly sovereign, since it is a relationship which requires no meritocratic middleman to make the connection, no elite representatives to give it effect. Popular loyalty and reverence for the monarchy is something given or not given by each citizen, acting according to the dictates of his heart.

It is, I think, impossible to exaggerate this element of sheer popular self-interest in the success of the monarchy – the extent to which the people go on sustaining it in glory and splendour so as to be able to go on enjoying the act of sustaining it in glory and splendour, which reflects as much glory on them as on the monarchy. It is a cooperative exercise, with the people positively insisting on maintaining the privileges of the monarchy, since the crucial role which they play in it is a vicarious way of sharing it. Only by loving royalty can they expect to be loved back by royalty, which is to say that only by building up a supreme figure to love can they hope to enjoy the pleasure of being loved by a supreme figure. 'Reciprocal complementary' is the sociologist's name for the game, and in Britain it is a game which the two players, monarchy and people, have now been playing for so long, with such proven skill, that maximum mutual satisfaction can be virtually guaranteed.

It can be argued of course that, since the monarchy does not govern, the fact that it depends in this way on popular participation does not mean very much; or that in so far as ordinary people get satisfaction from this kind of power – street power, if you like – they will have less incentive to take part in more sophisticated forms of political participation or civic responsibility. But this, in my opinion, is to miss the point, since the participation involved in demonstrating loyalty to the Queen is different from, and in some ways superior to, the participation talked about so much by, for example, Mr Benn. His kind has to do with people making their will felt in respect of particular communal arrangements: how factories should be run, where new towns should be situated and so on. But demonstrating loyalty to the monarchy is a way of participating in the national way of life; of affirming faith in the national character; of celebrating the national history; of doing the equivalent in public affairs to what making love is in private affairs. The aim is more sacramental than utilitarian, and it is precisely because the monarchy is above party politics that it is uniquely satisfactory as a focus for participation of this fundamental kind, infinitely more satisfactory than any elected head of state, since the latter is either a party leader or the nominee of party leaders.

Not all monarchies can fulfil this role. Indeed most proved unsuited to it, which is why they were abolished. But the British monarchy still can, which is why it has not been abolished. And it still can, in my view, because it is, of all the democratic institutions, the closest to the people in a real sense, since remaining close to all the people is an absolute necessity for it, much more so than for the political parties.

Political parties are by their nature partial in their appeal, responsive to some sections of the people and unresponsive to others. Their aim is to win a majority. That, in practice, is the most that they can aim at. In no real sense, therefore, is a government based on party dependent on 'the people'. It is dependent on some of the people, in touch with some of the people, sometimes, but not always, with a majority. But in the real world it is much more interested in placating particular interests and in maintaining particular loyalties than in reflecting the wishes of 'the people'. In fact, party politicians – which is what our rulers have to be – are probably less in touch with general public opinion than are most ordinary citizens because politicians' activity almost demands that they should not be: that they should be in touch only with party opinion. The party political view therefore is inevitably astigmatic, seeing deeper and farther into some areas of the public mind than others. Nor is this true only of party politicians. It is also true of those who write about politics, and of those who deal closely with politicians, since it is scarcely possible to do so without taking sides, which means under--standing one camp better than the others and seeing society largely, if not exclusively, from that particular angle of vision.

No, I am not suggesting – which would be absurd – that the royal family is closer to the people than are party politicians in the sense of having a better knowledge of their views about all the pressing material issues of the day. Palace life, after all, is not exactly best suited to induce much day-to-day understanding of the kind of problems felt most strongly by ordinary families. But then nor is life in Downing Street or the cushioned life lived by the socialist ideologues like Mr Crossman and Mr Crosland. By the time party politicians approach the levers of power, their way of life – chauffeur-driven cars, private secretaries to fetch and carry for them, etc. – has long since lost much contact with that of the man in the street.

What one means by being in touch, as far as the monarchy is concerned, is more a matter of properly reflecting the feelings of the people in relation to the particular function of being head of state. My contention would be that, whereas party politicians have allowed that part of the British political system for which they are responsible to grow steadily less and less in touch with what most people would wish it to be, to the point where it operates in a manner regarded as little short of scandalous by most citizens, the monarchy has adapted, stage by stage, in exactly the manner felt to be right and proper. Of what other British institution could this be said with equal truth? Take the civil service, for example, claiming and receiving index-linked pensions, which free its members from the worst effects of galloping inflation. Here is an example of a great national institution out of touch with the people. The same could be said of trade unions, which exercise their bargaining power in a manner deplored by public opinion; and of the City, which has also recently shown scant regard for the public's sense of what is right and wrong in the manipulation of money.

But the royal family, in the fields pertaining to its function, has not put a foot wrong, despite the many and obvious pitfalls in the path of an ancient monarchy in the modern world. It was urged, in the early 1950s, to become more democratic, by which was meant less stuffy and remote. But being relaxed and informal, unpompous and human, is not really the essence of the monarchical function. Like it or not – and if we don't like it, what is the point of having a royal family? – the attribute of majesty is the essence of monarchy. When all is said and done about the need for the royal family to develop the human touch, the fact remains that it is even more important to be able to wear a crown as if to the manner born, to *be* a king.

It has not been easy to get the balance right, and it seemed to me at one point that the royal family was in danger of being so successful in turning themselves into human beings that they would become increasingly ill-at-ease and unsuited to the occasions when they have to be primarily what they are intended to be: symbols of authority and majesty. In grey flannels and a tweed coat Prince Charles, for example, might seem perfectly comfortable. But put a crown on his head or an ermine cloak around his shoulders, and might the danger not be that he would look only a proper Charlie?

Then there was that famous BBC film in which the Queen spent a great deal of time posing for the television cameras as an ordinary mother of an ordinary family, picnicking in Deeside, buying sweets in the local shop, joking cosily around her private luncheon table, in all of which roles she seemed charmingly 'at home'. But could it be that all this propaganda, designed to create a royal style and manner better suited to enable royalty to mix with the people with less strain or embarrassment, might render them, for that very reason, less suited for the essential function of royalty, which involves being set apart and above the rest of mankind?

Or again, might not Prince Philip's accessibility to the media, in such marked contrast to the old remoteness, run the risk of involving the royal family in gaffes and indiscretions, from which the traditional protocol procedures were designed to protect it? These were real risks and dangers. But, with the benefit of hindsight, it is clear that the royal family were right to take them, since the monarchy does seem to have found the right balance.

Indeed, in the case of Prince Charles, they have done something rather more remarkable than produce a charming Prince. That, after all, given their advantages, would not be a particularly notable achievement. They have produced something which in 1977 is a much rarer phenomenon, with far more interesting social implications: a new variation of an historic species which was assumed to be as dead as the dodo, or, if not dead, to be found only on the music-hall stage as a figure of fun – an authentic, if one dare mention the word, gentleman.

Strangely enough, there is nothing very princely about his bearing, just as there is nothing very queenly about the bearing of his mother. In some ways all the ceremony and ritual in which he is involved, all the particularly royal parts of his life – the crown, orb and sceptre parts – seem somehow irrelevant, almost theatrical, blurring the contemporary royal message rather than underlining it. For what has caught the imagination about Prince Charles is his capacity not so much to play the Prince – that, as I say, is hardly surprising – but his ability to do something which nowadays is very difficult indeed, something which the old upper class in general has entirely lost the knack of: to exemplify in an acceptable manner the simple virtues of public service, filial duty, good manners, cheerfulness, individuality and a natural ease in social relationships born of being at peace with oneself and one's surroundings.

It is difficult to adjust our ideas of monarchy to such a relatively humdrum role. Its magic and mystery are still vaguely assumed to be generating something more marvellous than what used to be turned out in large numbers by tens of thousands of families. Let us be frank: a few years ago replicas of Prince Charles were being turned out *en masse*. But today they are not. The mould has somehow been broken. What is so marvellous to consider is the blessed fact that the mould has not been lost altogether, that the royal family has succeeded in preserving it, and has brought forth, just at the right moment, not a dazzling Prince – for which there is no need and no place – but a young man whose magnetism lies precisely in his being endowed with the ordinary qualities at a time when ordinary qualities are as rare as gold and as beautiful as works of art.

Perhaps only a royal family could have wrought this miracle, could have produced an offspring who can dare to be square. Uniquely immune from many of the contemporary pressures dissolving traditional standards of behaviour, cocooned from the more awful compulsions of precipitate social change, forced neither into the apologetic trendiness of an old ruling class on the wane, nor into the aggressive vulgarity of a new ruling class on the make, the royal family has been able to live an *ordinary* life – perhaps the only family in a position to do so – neither corroded by social guilt nor corrupted by social ambition, an ordinary natural life out of which has sprung a young man who amazes and delights not by being extraordinary in an ordinary world, but by being ordinary in an extraordinary world, by behaving naturally when all around him are behaving unnaturally, by being, it seems, at ease with his parents, with his role in society, at a time when the rest of us are lost in a maze of sham and confusion – by being, in a word, genuine in a counterfeit society.

This is the real magic of the monarchy today: that they are the family that has been least blown off course by all the current mumbo-jumbo of contemporary psychological quackery, least caught up in a social flux destroying their identity; that they are in truth much less mysterious, much less abnormal, much less peculiar than the rest of us. It is we, their subjects, who are living peculiar, abnormal, mysterious lives, circling, so to speak, in social outer space, out of touch with any recognizable reality, confused, uncertain, mixed-up, while they – which is what is really remarkable about them – still seem to have their feet on *terra firma*, still seem to know what they are about, still seem able to behave as human beings were meant to behave.

Compared with pop stars, student protesters, beatniks, pot-smokers and all the other weird forms of youth today, Prince Charles – even when dressed up in crown and ermine – is infinitely comprehensible. This surely is the secret of his impact.

In spite of all the pomp and pageantry with which he is surrounded, in spite of all the ritual through which he is led, there is an expression on his face and a smile on his lips which make him more human, and therefore more truly lovable, than all the other contemporary idols of youth, for all their supposedly swinging with-it-ness. How strange and rather wonderful it is that it should be the role of monarchy today not to act out phantasy but to be the one institution that seems able to be natural and normal.

That is what I mean by the monarchy being in touch with the people, since it seems to me that, in producing an heir to the throne so exactly right for the times, the royal family has shown a quality totally and tragically lacking in the other great national institutions: the ability to renew itself and secure its future in a manner at once original and reassuring, imaginative and traditional and, most important of all, uniquely, unmistakably British.

But will this be enough to preserve the monarchy in the coming years? Realism must preclude any complacent assumptions on this score, and lead one to predict dangerous tests not far ahead. For a divided society, with class pitted against class – as Britain is increasingly becoming – is likely to create unprecedented problems for a monarchy dedicated to the task of symbolizing national unity. For how can the monarchy symbolize something that does not exist? Or reflect a social consensus which is increasingly challenged? Or, as an institution wholly outside politics, preside satisfactorily over a society which is becoming ever more politicized?

Quite recently, for example, the Duke of Edinburgh made a speech in praise of initiative, thrift, hard work, self-sufficiency, only to be accused by the Labour left of interfering in politics. And this is bound to be a recurring complaint as the government becomes responsible for an ever widening area of the nation's life, since there will scarcely be any area left which is not a matter of party controversy. If the Duke were to speak out in favour of social justice, he would be attacked by the Conservative right for favouring socialism. Education, medicine, town planning, penology, even charity are now politically divisive issues. Given the new arguments about morality, it will soon be an interference in politics to be against sin or in favour of sex.

But the most perilous development of all is the looming threat of a conflict between the state and the trade unions. If there were to be industrial confrontation with the next Conservative government, to the point where the army were called in by the civil power to break a strike in the essential services, a situation little short of civil war cannot altogether be ruled out. It is precisely in such grave circumstances that a head of state might have a crucial role to play, since the party system could well collapse under the strain. But, precisely because a monarchy in modern times is the most non-political form of head of state, the least suited – for obvious reasons – to play any part in such a crisis, it could be argued that at the moment of the country's greatest need it will be tried and found wanting, found wanting in the sense of being too fearful of getting its hands dirtied.

Or alternatively, it could be argued that it would get involved, but in a way that would turn organized labour against it, thus imperilling its future. The close and intimate ties between the Crown and the armed services – ties forged by history – would undoubtedly be a major factor in this kind of scenario, since the willingness of the armed services to be used might well be determined by the monarch's attitude to the risks involved. These apocalyptic possibilities have only to be mentioned for the perils lying in wait for the monarchy to be readily understood. But they are perils which affirm the unique and continuing potency of the institution, since on the person of no other non-elected head of state in the world, in a comparable crisis, would so much depend – for good or ill.

The Queen's Subjects

THE QUEEN

There she sits upon the throne. She does not rule over Britain in any way she just sits there every day. She just sits there every day not happily not sad just sitting there every day.

Stephen Jones

THE QUEEN
(*why I hate her*)

I hate the Queen because she is a Snob who always goes around doing important things without a smile on her face. She does not even give money to the poor and that is sheer measliness. She also talks like a cat. She always goes to meetings and always buts in on other peoples Conversations. She also dresses up in clothes and goes to *Balls* all the time.

Steven Quirke

This is why I like the Queen because she is not big headed or selfish and she try to help other people. And she goes to other country and give money to good cause and the same in Britain plus she is head of state. And she as not done nothing to me.

Paul Shaw

185

The Queen

Queen in a diamond Crown.
Upon Buckingham place lives the queen.
Europe the queen travels.
Emrald the queens ring.
Name the queen, queen Elizabeth.

England the queen repersants.
Long and Gold dress, the queen wears.
I Promise to Pay the Bearer on Demand the sum of £1
Zoo's impress the queen.
April the Queen's birthday.
Beefeaters guard Buckinham place.
Event's the queen will travel for Great B.
Through-out the years the queen will live.
Happy ever after the queen should live.

Ranjodh Singh

WHAT I WOULD DO IF THE QUEEN COME TO SEE ME

What I would do if the queen come to see me is I would do all the washing up, wash the kitchen floor sweep all the carpets wash all the paint work down I washed the windows and all the paintwork outside. I made all the beds and I tided the bath room up. I put some money in the meater so the lights would not go off half way frow the dinner. I got some bone china cups and sosers and I borght some new nifes and forkes and I holyed the kitchen and I put chiken in the oven and all over hung what go with a rost and then I would put on my best suit and shirt and tie and I would by some roses for her and a rose for my butten hole.

Paul Pitchley

13/40